MID-CONTINENT PUBLIC LIBRARY
15616 E. 24 HWY
INDEPENDENCE

D1467120

WITHDRAWN
FROM THE RECORDS OF THE
MID-CONTINENT PUBLIC LIBRARY

SPECIAL MESSAGE TO READERS

THE ULVERSCROFT FOUNDATION
(registered UK charity number 264873)
was established in 1972 to provide funds for
research, diagnosis and treatment of eye diseases.
Examples of major projects funded by
the Ulverscroft Foundation are:-

- The Children's Eye Unit at Moorfields Eye Hospital, London
- The Ulverscroft Children's Eye Unit at Great Ormond Street Hospital for Sick Children
- Funding research into eye diseases and treatment at the Department of Ophthalmology, University of Leicester
- The Ulverscroft Vision Research Group, Institute of Child Health
- Twin operating theatres at the Western Ophthalmic Hospital, London
- The Chair of Ophthalmology at the Royal Australian College of Ophthalmologists

You can help further the work of the Foundation
by making a donation or leaving a legacy.
Every contribution is gratefully received. If you
would like to help support the Foundation or
require further information, please contact:

THE ULVERSCROFT FOUNDATION
The Green, Bradgate Road, Anstey
Leicester LE7 7FU, England
Tel: (0116) 236 4325
website: www.foundation.ulverscroft.com

THE RETURN OF
SHERLOCK HOLMES

Though Professor Moriarty has perished at the Reichenbach Falls, Sherlock Holmes must still pit his wits against his old and deadly enemies — the malevolent blackmailer Charles Augustus Milverton, and the murderous Colonel Sebastian Moran . . . In this collection the author also gives us another of his own fictional creations: the sardonic Martin Brett — a more modern equivalent of the great detective — in four further ingenious stories of murder and mystery.

ERNEST DUDLEY

THE RETURN OF SHERLOCK HOLMES

Complete and Unabridged

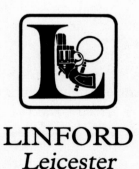

LINFORD
Leicester

First published in Great Britain

First Linford Edition
published 2013

Copyright © 1951. 1994 by Ernest Dudley
Copyright © 2012 by Susan Dudley Allen
All rights reserved

*A catalogue record for this book is available
from the British Library.*

ISBN 978–1–4448–1761–4

Published by
F. A. Thorpe (Publishing)
Anstey, Leicestershire

Set by Words & Graphics Ltd.
Anstey, Leicestershire
Printed and bound in Great Britain by
T. J. International Ltd., Padstow, Cornwall

This book is printed on acid-free paper

THE RETURN OF
SHERLOCK HOLMES

1

Cold autumn midday sunshine slanted into a room in Dr. Shlessinger's London nursing home. It was a clinical-looking room, with white walls, centrally located French windows with net curtains, and plain-coloured curtains. It was furnished with a writing desk, table, and chairs. On one side was a door from the hall, and on the opposite wall was a half-open second door that led to the laboratory.

Lady Frances Carfax lay in an easy chair. She was beautiful, but pale. Her eyes were closed, as if asleep. Through the laboratory doorway Cecilia Shlessinger could be seen as she worked. She was attractive in a rather cold way, 30ish, and wearing a smart nurse's uniform.

Lady Frances suddenly woke up and cried out: 'Oh — oh, my God! No — no! Nurse Cecilia!'

At the anguished call Cecilia came

hurrying out of the laboratory. 'All right, Lady Frances . . . '

'Quickly — quickly!'

Cecilia reached Lady Frances's side. 'What is it?'

Lady Frances was now fully awake. 'I've had a terrible nightmare. I was being attacked by . . . '

The nurse took her hand, and sought to calm her. 'You're all right now. You're quite safe.'

Lady Frances gave a little shudder. 'It was a man . . . a big man . . . he was dressed like . . . like . . . ' She shook her head. 'He was going to kill me . . . yet he was smiling and friendly.'

'No one is going to kill you,' Cecilia soothed.

'But he was! While he was smiling, and he had on this . . . this black coat . . . '

The nurse smiled. 'It was just a silly nightmare, I tell you. Now, just stay quiet — and I'll bring you your medicine.'

'He was a big man — and smiling — '

'Yes, yes. Just you lie quiet.' Cecilia hurried back to the laboratory.

Lady Frances called after her: 'Is it

more of that horrid medicine?'

'No, no. This will be much nicer,' the nurse said reassuringly. 'I promise you.'

'You're sure?' Lady Frances asked doubtfully.

'Quite sure. My brother's made it nicer to taste.' The nurse came out of the laboratory with a small tray holding a medicine glass, a small jug of water and a medicine phial. She placed them on a table beside Lady Frances, who looked at the tray doubtfully.

The nurse poured medicine into a glass, then after adding a little water she handed it to Lady Frances.

She took the glass somewhat reluctantly. 'Are you sure it's a nicer taste?'

The nurse nodded. 'I promise you it is.'

Lady Frances drank the medicine and gave a little shudder. 'Ugh! It's horrible . . . horrible!'

She returned the glass to Cecilia, who put it back on the tray, turned, and hurried with it to the laboratory.

Lady Frances took a sweet from her handbag and quickly popped it into her mouth. 'Even the sweet doesn't take away the taste. I'm sure this new doctor my brother's got for me won't prescribe such horrid stuff.'

Cecilia stood in the laboratory doorway, and stared at Lady Frances with a frozen expression. 'No, Lady Frances,' she said tightly.

Lady Frances looked up. Instantly the nurse's expression changed. 'What did you say his name is . . . Dr. — Dr. Wilson?'

'Watson,' Cecilia corrected.

'Dr. Watson . . . that's right! Well, I hope he'll have something to say about my medicine.'

At that moment, a grim-faced man entered from the hall. Dr. Shlessinger was a big man, wearing striped trousers with a black morning coat. As Lady Frances turned to look at him, his expression changed as he quickly adopted a benevolent, 'bedside' attitude.

He gave a quick nod to Cecilia, who closed the laboratory door behind her and waited.

He came straight across the room where Lady Frances sat in her easy chair.

'Good morning, Lady Frances,' he smiled expansively.

'Oh, Doctor! The medicine's horrible . . . ' Lady Frances complained. 'Even worse than before!'

Shlessinger glanced across to Cecilia. 'You are serving our patient the correct dose, of course?'

The nurse gave a little shrug. 'Yes, I'm following your instructions precisely,' she answered formally. Then, with a curt nod to Lady Frances, she crossed the room and went out into the hall.

Shlessinger turned to Lady Frances and looked at her reassuringly. 'Now, Lady Frances, you wanted to see me. About . . . ?'

Lady Frances appeared to pull herself together. Reaching for her handbag, she took out a letter from it. She looked up at the doctor.

'Your sister says this came by hand, last night,' she said briefly.

Shlessinger nodded. 'Yes, that's so,' he assented.

Lady Frances glanced down at the letter. She appeared deeply upset. 'It's

7

from . . . from Philip Green. I've tried to read it, but I can't believe what it says. Read it to me, please.' She handed letter to Shlessinger.

'I'm sorry it has upset you so much,' the doctor murmured, taking the letter.

Lady Frances dabbed at her eyes. 'He says he doesn't want to see me again.

'I'm sure he can't mean that.'

Lady Frances sniffed. 'Read it for yourself.'

'If you wish,' Shlessinger said, with every appearance of reluctance. He read the letter aloud:

' 'My dear: If I have given you cause to believe I cherish feelings for you that are more than friendship' . . . ' He broke off as Lady Frances interjected:

'We were engaged to be married.'

Shlessinger paused respectfully for a moment, then continued reading:

' 'I am deeply sorry. I feel it better for us both that we should not meet again. Before you receive this, I shall have gone away. Please forgive me. Philip Green'.'

Lady Frances began to sob gently.

'I can't believe it. I won't believe it . . . '

Shlessinger gave her a sympathetic smile. 'I'm sure Mr. Green will realize he has made a dreadful mistake and will want to return to you.' He handed the letter back to Lady Frances, who agitatedly crumpled it in her hand.

He paused, then added hesitantly: 'There is a postscript that I . . . er . . . didn't read . . . '

Lady Frances looked up sharply. 'Postscript? What does it say?'

'Really, I . . . er . . . ' Shlessinger spoke awkwardly. ' . . . I think it is only for your eyes, dear lady.'

Lady Frances looked down at the letter clutched in her hand and slowly smoothed it out. In a low voice she read: ' 'As for the bonds, I intend to hang on to them. No one will know where they are'.' Tightening her lips, she crushed the letter again and threw it to the floor with a shudder of disgust. Then turned in appeal to Shlessinger.

'You will never mention this to anyone — ever. Please. I forbid you.'

'Very well,' Shlessinger murmured.

Lady Frances sighed, getting a grip on

her emotions. 'Now, there's something else,' she said hesitatingly. 'My brother, I'm afraid, isn't satisfied with my progress.'

'I'm very concerned to hear that,' Shlessinger said, frowning slightly.

'He was here yesterday, and — '

Shlessinger gave a start. 'Lord Henry called here?'

'Yesterday afternoon,' Lady Frances affirmed. 'And he insisted — '

She broke off as Cecilia entered from the hall.

'Dr. Watson is here, Lady Frances,' she announced. 'Forgive me for interrupting.'

Shlessinger gave a start. 'Doctor . . . Watson? Who . . . ?'

'Lady Frances's new doctor,' Cecilia told him calmly.

'I was about to explain,' Lady Frances put in.

'Dr. Watson, did you say?' Shlessinger still appeared disconcerted.

'I've taken him to your room,' Cecilia told Lady Frances. 'He's waiting for you.'

'Very well, I'll go along.' Cecilia helped her to rise and then escorted Lady

Frances out. She looked at her gratefully. 'Thank you. Perhaps Dr. Watson will get me well soon, and I'll be able to manage by myself.'

Cecilia glanced back over her shoulder and gave Shlessinger a warning look, then turned to Lady Frances and smiled. 'I'm sure he will.'

Getting Cecilia's message, Shlessinger got a grip on himself. 'Yes, of course, I'm sure he will,' he called after them.

After they had gone Shlessinger stood in the middle of the room, scowling and muttering to himself. 'Dr. Watson? It can't be . . . '

He broke off as he thought he heard a sound outside the French windows. He started to go across to them, then stopped and shook his head, still muttering to himself. 'No. No, it can't be; all the same, something's wrong.' Going over to the door he looked after Cecilia and Lady Frances for a moment, then turned back to the centre of room. 'First the damn brother and now . . . ' He spun and looked to the doorway as Cecilia returned.

'What's been happening?' he demanded.

'Who's this Dr. Watson?

'Keep your voice down,' Cecilia admonished him.

Shlessinger was still angry. 'Not only do you let Lord Henry see her . . . '

Cecilia spread her hands. 'He called out of the blue. I couldn't shut the door in his face, could I?'

Shlessinger calmed slightly. 'And now this Dr. Watson — do you realize he must be an imposter?'

Cecilia shook her head.

'No, it's the real one.'

'But it can't be,' Shlessinger protested. 'He hasn't been heard of since Sherlock Holmes' death in Switzerland.'

Cecilia remained adamant. 'I tell you . . . ' she broke off as the doorbell rang. 'That'll be Milverton.' She crossed to the door and turned to look back before going on into the hall to admit the caller. 'You're expecting him. He'll tell you about Dr. Watson.'

Shlessinger exhaled violently. 'This is supposed to be a quiet nursing home. It's more like Paddington Station,' he muttered, and began pacing up and down.

Suddenly he paused, going over to the French windows again, and staring out. He failed to see anything, and turned as he heard Cecilia talking to Milverton as she admitted him into the house.

A few moments later Milverton and Cecilia came into the room.

Milverton was a man of about 50, with a perpetual frozen smile. His keen eyes gleamed brightly behind horn-rimmed glasses. He was wearing a morning suit of perfect cut, and a fur-lined overcoat with collar and cuffs of astrakhan. He was carrying his hat in his hand. He waited, smiling at Shlessinger.

'Mr. Milverton, for Dr. Shlessinger,' Cecilia said, formally.

'Good morning, my dear Doctor,' the newcomer said affably, his voice smooth and suave. 'Charles Augustus Milverton at your service. Charmed to . . . '

Shlessinger ignored his visitor's extended hand. 'All right,' he said sourly, 'cut the soft soap . . . save it for your victims.'

Cecilia smiled thinly. 'I'll leave you two to chat.' She turned and went out

'Victims?' Milverton gave an imperturbable smile. 'Victims?' he repeated, beaming. 'I may be called the greatest scoundrel in London, the mere sound of my name may cause many to blanch, but then, as I try to reassure them, I do you no harm — on the contrary, I protect you against harm, danger, disgrace. So long as you continue to contribute a reasonable sum at intervals convenient to you . . .'

Shlessinger waved a deprecating hand. 'All right. But what's this about Dr. Watson?'

Milverton shrugged. 'Well, what about him?'

'He's the friend of the late Mr. Sherlock Holmes, who I thought had disappeared without trace. He's here attending our patient.'

'You haven't got it quite right,' Milverton said quietly.

'It's what Cecilia's just told me,' Shlessinger insisted. 'I say he's an imposter.'

'What I mean,' Milverton explained patiently, 'is that Sherlock Holmes is no

14

longer 'the late'; on the contrary he's very much alive.'

'What?' Shlessinger was clearly shocked. 'But . . . but he went over the Reichenbach Falls with Moriarty — '

Milverton nodded. 'That's what was *supposed* to have happened. But though Moriarty died, Holmes survived.'

'My God . . . Sherlock Holmes, alive!' Shlessinger appeared shattered by the news.

'No need to let it worry you,' Milverton assured him.

'Worry me? Don't you see what's going on?' He paused to follow Shlessinger's gaze and saw that Cecilia had come back into the room. 'So it *is* Dr. Watson,' he went on. 'Sent to spy on us by Sherlock Holmes.'

Seeing her brother's evident agitation, Cecilia glanced at Milverton. 'Have you given him the good news?'

'I was coming to that,' Milverton said.

Shlessinger looked at him sharply. 'Good news?'

'Colonel Moran is taking care of Holmes,' Milverton told him complacently.

As realization dawned, Shlessinger gave a grim smile, visibly relaxing. 'Moran! Moriarty's closest friend?'

Milverton nodded. 'And who is determined to avenge his death.'

'So you've nothing to worry about,' Cecilia added.

'You can forget Sherlock Holmes,' Milverton told Shlessinger. 'Lady Frances is all you need concern yourself with.'

'But what about her brother?' Shlessinger said, looking at Cecilia.

The woman shrugged. 'He's out of the way now. Zurich, urgent business. He went last night, so . . . '

'Which brings me to the matter of the letter,' Milverton interposed. He took a letter from his inside pocket and handed it to Shlessinger. 'Just check that it's the same as the fake her ladyship received.'

Shlessinger took the letter and began to read bits of it aloud: ''My dear, If I have given you cause to believe . . . I shall have gone away . . . please' . . . ' He returned the letter to Milverton. 'It's identical,' he grunted.

'Postscript and all,' Milverton said complacently.

'Postscript and all,' Shlessinger agreed.

Milverton pocketed the letter and smiled. 'My speciality.'

Cecilia looked at their visitor. 'Any trouble with her ex-fiancé?' she asked.

'The Colonel's looking after him, all right,' Milverton said confidently. He turned to Shlessinger, adding: 'Now, to business. I need five minutes with your patient, that's what I'm here for.'

Cecilia spread her hands 'Dr. Watson's with her at the moment.'

'Damn the man!' Shlessinger snapped.

'Look, why not leave her a note?' Cecilia suggested. 'Say it's urgent, and that you'll come back this afternoon.'

'Good idea!' Milverton nodded. He went over to the writing desk and, using his fountain pen, began writing on the notepaper he found already on the desk.

'I'll see she gets your note,' Cecilia said.

Milverton looked up. 'What time shall I say I'll be here?'

Cecilia thought for a moment. 'Say three. I'll fix it.'

17

Milverton finished the letter, placed it into an envelope, and sealed it. He handed it to Cecilia. 'I haven't signed it 'Milverton', of course. I've called myself Tamworth . . . George Tamworth.'

Cecilia nodded. 'Of course, 'Mr. Tamworth'.'

Unseen by the three in the room, a tall figure momentarily flitted past the French window.

'If there's any hitch,' Milverton said, considering, 'if she can't see me . . . telephone me . . . '

'I'll make sure she sees you,' Cecilia assured him.

'There's no time to lose,' Shlessinger said.

'Back at three, then.' Milverton crossed to the door and went out, followed by Cecilia.

Frowning, Shlessinger looked back and at the French windows and hesitated.

'Come along,' Cecilia told him sharply. 'We'd better see how Dr. Watson is getting on with our patient.'

Shlessinger continued looking at the French windows for a moment, listening intently, then gave a shrug and turned away. 'All right, just coming. Thought I heard someone in the garden, but there's no one.'

A few moments after they'd left the room, the fleeting tall figure appeared again outside. Suddenly Shlessinger returned, and stood in the doorway, looking again at the French windows.

But the figure had gone. Shlessinger waited a moment, then with a shake of his head, turned and went out again. As he did so, the figure reappeared outside.

There came a click of a lock being turned and Sherlock Holmes entered the room. He was wearing an ordinary suit and hat. Quickly crossing to Lady Frances's chair, he picked up the crumpled letter she had thrown down. He pocketed it and then, going quickly to the laboratory door, he opened it and entered. A moment later Holmes came out of the laboratory with a phial, which he glanced at before slipping it into his pocket. He shut and relocked the laboratory door.

He paused as he heard Lady Frances

and Dr. Watson speaking in the hall. Turning back into the centre of room, he took off his hat and awaited their arrival.

Seeing the tall figure of Sherlock Holmes as she entered, Lady Frances gave a violent start

'Who are you?' she demanded.

'Holmes!' Watson exclaimed as he followed her into the room. 'But no one said you were here!'

'That is because I took good care that no one should know.'

'This is Mr. Sherlock Holmes,' Watson introduced hastily, as Lady Frances continued staring at Holmes, who gave her a little bow.

'How do you do, Lady Frances?' Holmes said, smiling.

Watson glanced at Lady Frances. 'As I explained, your brother had a word with Mr. Holmes after his visit here.'

'And he seems to think I can be of help to you . . . over a certain matter,' Holmes told her.

Lady Frances frowned at him. 'I know I agreed to Dr. Watson's being here, but I didn't think . . . ' She broke off as

Shlessinger strode into the room, leaving the door ajar.

'Lady Frances,' he began immediately, 'I wonder if . . . ' He stopped as he saw Holmes. Instinctively, he pretended not to recognise him. 'Who's this? Who are you, sir?'

'My name is Sherlock Holmes, Dr. Shlessinger,' Holmes said evenly.

'You have the advantage of me, sir,' Shlessinger lied. 'But how did you get in here?'

'Mr. Holmes is here at Lord Henry's request,' Dr. Watson interposed quickly.

Lady Frances sighed. 'I know my brother is interfering but, since he is my brother, with my welfare at heart . . . '

Holmes called out, interrupting her: 'Do come in, Miss Shlessinger. You're causing a slight draught, from which I'm sure you wouldn't want your patient to suffer.'

Cecilia, who had indeed been listening behind the door her brother had left open, pushed it further open and came into the room.

'Like my brother, I thought you were

dea — ' She broke off quickly as she saw her brother's glare. 'I'm so sorry, please forgive me.'

'I fancied a certain Mr. Milverton brought you news that reports of my demise have been grossly exaggerated?' Holmes told her challengingly.

'Milverton?' Shlessinger kept up his pretence. 'I don't believe we know anyone of that name.'

Holmes raised an eyebrow. 'Charles Augustus Milverton?'

Shlessinger looked at his sister. 'Can you recall a Mr. Milverton, my dear?'

'Not really . . . no. Milverton, did you say?'

'Almost the greatest scoundrel in London,' Holmes said dryly.

'Of course, we've never heard of such a person,' Shlessinger blustered.

Cecilia looked defiantly at Holmes. 'I really can't think of anyone.'

Holmes smiled cynically. 'Yet only a few minutes ago, in this very room, the three of you were discussing a matter of supreme importance to not only to yourselves, but also Lady Frances.'

A nonplussed expression gusted over Shlessinger's face. Then he glanced from Holmes to the French windows and realized it had been Holmes he'd heard outside. He continued to try and bluff his way out. 'What are you saying?' He turned to Watson. 'Really, Dr. Watson, your friend . . . '

Lady Frances looked at Shlessinger fixedly. 'Is this true?' she demanded. 'That you were discussing me with Mr. — Mr. — ?'

'I assure you that Mr. Holmes is imagining things,' Shlessinger said.

Lady Frances swung her gaze back to Holmes. 'You seem to know something which I don't! What has my brother been telling you?'

'He believes you to be in some danger,' Holmes told her.

Shlessinger bridled. 'Danger? What nonsense! Why — ' he stopped as Cecilia tugged at his arm.

Lady Frances turned to Dr. Watson. 'But I'm not really ill, you said.'

'Dear Lady Frances,' Cecilia said insinuatingly, 'I'm so sorry you're being distressed in this way.'

Lady Frances wavered. 'What should I do, Dr. Watson?' she appealed to him.

Watson spoke firmly. 'Perhaps you should listen to what Mr. Holmes has to say.'

Lady Frances looked again at Cecilia, then Shlessinger, who glanced at Cecilia. His sister gave a little shrug.

'No doubt Mr. Holmes is anxious to earn the fat fee he's been paid,' she said. 'I suggest that we allow him to try his best.' She signalled to her brother: 'Come along, my dear.'

'Very well.' Shlessinger spoke reluctantly. He looked coldly at Holmes. 'Perhaps you'll be good enough to let us know when you're ready to leave.'

Lady Frances turned to Watson as he brought forth a chair and invited her to sit down.

Cecilia smiled at her sympathetically and turned to leave, followed by Shlessinger.

'A moment, Miss Shlessinger,' Holmes said sharply. The Shlessingers stopped and turned to him. Holmes extended his right hand. 'The letter, please. May I see it?'

They glanced at each other, then at Holmes, as if mystified.

'Letter? What letter?' Shlessinger blustered.

'Letter, Mr. Holmes?' Cecilia frowned.

Holmes crossed to her, continuing to hold his hand extended.

Cecilia gave him a frozen smile.

'If you please?' Holmes said firmly.

Cecilia affected to suddenly realize to what Holmes had been referring to. 'Oh, that letter.'

Shlessinger became alarmed. 'What is it? Some prescription or something? Give it here.' He held out his hand.

'Isn't it addressed to Lady Frances?' Holmes said sharply. Cecilia hesitated momentarily, then shrugged and gave the letter to Lady Frances.

She started to open it, then handed it to Dr. Watson. 'You read it for me, Dr. Watson, please.'

Watson glanced at Holmes, who gave a nod. He took the letter and opened it. After a quick scan, he summarized its contents:

'It is from a Mr. Tamworth, requesting an appointment. He says it's something very confidential about which he can help you.'

Lady Frances frowned. 'But who is Mr. Tamworth? I don't know anyone of that name.'

'Perhaps I may explain,' Holmes interposed crisply. ' "Tamworth" is an alias adopted by the aforementioned Mr. Milverton, who happens to be a notorious blackmailer!'

Lady Frances looked aghast. 'A blackmailer?' she whispered.

Holmes continued his revelations. 'Criminals when choosing an alias, invariably pick a name which has some connection with the crime they are planning.' He paused, and then addressed a question to Shlessinger, who, with Cecilia, had been pretending to look shocked. 'What is this address, by the way?'

'Address? Address . . . ' Shlessinger looked at his sister. 'What does he mean?'

'It's the Laurels Nursing Home, *Tamworth* Road, of course.' Watson pointed out dryly.

Holmes nodded. 'You see, Mr. Milverton runs true to form in his choice of another name.'

'But what am I to do?' Lady Frances faltered.

Shlessinger attempted a bluff. 'I think we should fetch the police — ' he glared at Holmes — 'unless you leave at once.'

Lady Frances became alarmed. 'Police! No, no, that's the last thing you must do.'

Holmes smiled sardonically. 'Believe me, Lady Frances, it is the last thing he will do.'

'Don't be too sure of that,' Shlessinger snapped. He turned to his sister. 'Come along, my dear, we . . . we must consult our solicitors about this matter.' He took her arm.

Cecilia allowed herself to be led from the room. 'Yes, yes, of course, our solicitors . . . '

'Sue for slander, that's what we'll do . . . ' Shlessinger muttered as they went out.

Holmes moved over to where Lady Frances was sitting dazedly on the chair

Watson had provided.

'Now, Lady Frances, I'd like to look at your hands.' He glanced at Watson who was hovering solicitously at her side. 'Dr. Watson?'

Watson nodded as Lady Frances looked at him. 'Mr. Holmes is an authority on poisons.'

'Poisons?' She extended her hands quickly.

Holmes examined them carefully.

'The medicine you took a short while ago ... ' he murmured, raising an interrogative eyebrow,

'Which Nurse Shlessinger gave me?' Lady Frances asked, her voice wavering.

Holmes nodded. 'It made you feel cold?'

'Yes, very cold ... deathly ... as I told Dr. Watson ... '

'I've changed the prescription, of course.' Watson said promptly.

'And rather dizzy?' Holmes continued, releasing her hands.

'Yes. I couldn't think properly.'

'What you have been taking,' Holmes explained, 'was administered to you for the precise purpose of weakening your willpower, preparatory for an attempt at blackmail.'

Lady Frances stared at him in disbelief. 'Blackmail? My God!' She swung to Watson. 'Is . . . is this true?'

'I'm afraid so.'

'You have been the victim of a deliberate plot,' Holmes told her. 'But fortunately, your brother suspected, and came to Watson.'

'You mean, Dr . . . Dr. Shlessinger and his sister . . . ?' Lady Frances whispered.

' . . . are notorious criminals, who intend to bleed you of every penny you possess!' Holmes finished bluntly.

'Oh!' Lady Frances slumped in her chair.

Watson took her hands comfortingly. 'You are safe now. Absolutely out of danger.'

'What . . . what had the man with the two names got to do with all this?' Lady Frances asked.

'I will explain everything later,' Holmes assured her. His tone became urgent. 'But now, we must get you away from here.'

'But where shall I go?'

'An hotel, where your brother has arranged for you to stay,' Holmes told her. 'You can stay there until all this has blown over.' He pointed to the French windows. 'Dr. Watson will see you safely by way of the garden. I've got a cab waiting.' He glanced at his watch. 'It's all according to plan.'

Watson and Lady Frances followed Holmes to the French windows.

He was just opening the windows for them when Shlessinger and Cecilia came into the room. Shlessinger strode forward angrily.

'What the devil's going on?'

'They're kidnapping our patient,' Cecilia commented.

Holmes ushered Watson and Lady Frances out into the garden. 'Hurry, hurry . . . '

When they had gone he closed the windows and turned calmly back into the room.

'Damn your eyes!' Shlessinger snarled.

Holmes tapped his pocket where he'd put the phial taken from the laboratory.

'I've got here the poison you were giving to Lady Frances. Evidence enough to jail you both.'

'The phial! He's got the phial!' Cecilia screeched furiously.

Cecilia following, Shlessinger lunged forward, his hands extended. 'You can't think you'll get away with this!'

They halted in their tracks as Holmes suddenly produced a small revolver from his other pocket. 'Put your hands up!' he snapped.

Shlessinger started to obey, but Cecilia resumed moving forward.

'It's only a toy!' she cried. 'He's bluffing! Stop him!'

Shlessinger moved towards Holmes, only to halt abruptly as the detective fired a shot at his feet.

'My God!' Shlessinger shouted. 'He'll kill us!'

'I shan't warn you again,' Holmes said evenly. 'Hands up and keep them up!'

This time both Shlessinger and his sister obeyed. Keeping them covered and forcing them back, Holmes crossed quickly to the open door. Still keeping

31

them covered, he took out the key from it with his free hand. At that moment a loud taxi-hoot sounded from the street.

'Just coming!' Holmes murmured, darting out and slamming the door after him.

Shlessinger and Cecilia rushed towards the door, then halted as they heard the key turning in the lock.

Shlessinger began wrenching at the door handle. 'He's locked us in! You'll pay for this, Holmes!' he shouted.

'Yes!' Cecilia screeched in rage. 'Colonel Moran will see to that. D'you hear, Mr. Bloody Sherlock Holmes? Moran'll settle your hash!'

She quivered with rage as another taxi-hoot sounded outside.

2

It was late in the afternoon on the same day as Sherlock Holmes and Dr. Watson had contrived the rescue of Lady Frances Carfax from Shlessinger's Nursing Home. Holmes had just finished tea in his comfortable room on the first floor at his Baker Street home. He pushed back his chair and lighted his pipe, looking about him.

A telephone projected from the wall beside the door leading to the landing outside it. A warm fire crackled in the fireplace against the back wall. From the coal scuttle protruded a box of cigars, a Persian slipper serving for a tobacco jar. Holmes' reflective gaze travelled to the window, overlooking Baker Street, then along the bookshelves lining the far wall. In front of them was a writing desk littered with papers, pipes and odds and ends, on which had been thrown a violin and bow. On either side of the desk were two shabby but comfortable armchairs. A mass of correspondence for attention was pinned to a bookshelf by a jackknife.

Footsteps sounded from the landing outside, followed by a gentle but firm knock on the door.

'Come in,' Holmes called. His house-keeper entered, carrying a tray. 'Thank you, Mrs. Hudson,' he added, as the woman deftly placed his tea-things on the tray.

Just as she turned to go out, the front door bell rang. Holmes glanced at his watch and frowned slightly.

'Now, who could that be?' Mrs. Hudson said. She left to answer the summons, taking the tray with her.

'Dr. Watson's probably forgotten his key,' Holmes murmured as she went out.

'Not like him to do that,' Mrs. Hudson commented over her shoulder. Still carrying the tray as she went downstairs she called out, 'All right, Doctor, I'm coming.'

Holmes put down his pipe and crossed to the writing desk, where he picked up his violin. Downstairs, after setting aside her tray, Mrs. Hudson opened the front door.

'Inspector Lestrade?' she exclaimed in surprise. 'I thought it was . . . '

'Afternoon, Mrs. H.,' Lestrade greeted her in his brisk cockney accent, full of self-importance. 'And how are you?

Hearing the exchange through his open door, Holmes put down his violin and returned to the table, his manner alert. 'Lestrade?' he muttered to himself. 'What can he want?'

Mrs. Hudson called up the stairs. 'It's Inspector Lestrade, Mr. Holmes.'

'Lestrade of the Yard,' he called after her.

Mrs. Hudson regarded him quizzically. 'You usually give three short, sharp rings, Inspector.'

'Ah, that's when I'm expected, Mrs. H.,' Lestrade smiled. 'I wasn't this time, you see.'

He looked up as Holme's voice sounded from the top of the stairs.

'Come on up, Inspector.'

Lestrade lost no time in hurrying

upstairs, and into Holmes' room.

'Good afternoon, Mr. Holmes.' Lestrade had come in plain clothes, and was wearing a dark overcoat. Putting his bowler hat on the table, he shook hands with Holmes.

'Good afternoon, Inspector. This is an unexpected pleasure.'

'I'll get down to business straight away,' the Inspector said. 'It's to do with Colonel Moran.'

Holmes raised an eyebrow. 'Moran?'

'He's in London,' Lestrade said urgently.

'Is he now?'

'And seeing as how his purpose in being here concerns you directly, I thought you should know.'

'Many thanks, indeed.'

'My information,' Lestrade went on, 'is that he's got that special gun of his with him.' He looked at Holmes grimly.

'The walking-stick gun?'

'The very same what blew young Ronald Adair's head clean off his shoulders.' Lestrade gave a shudder. 'Made even me — who's seen a few nasty sights in his time — feel sick in the stomach.'

Holmes nodded gravely. 'It's a murderous weapon, I agree.'

'And I'm sure I don't have to tell you who he plans to aim it at this time. He's obsessed that you killed his pal, Moriarty.'

'You have my full attention, Inspector,' Holmes told him.

'I'm here to warn you to find yourself a quiet little country pub and lie low until I give you the tip-off that I've got Moran safely behind bars.' Lestrade's tone indicated his confidence in his own ability to bring the notorious criminal to book.

Holmes was unconvinced. 'But on what charge? You weren't able to nab him over the Adair case, though both you and I knew he was as guilty as hell.'

'He's behind a blackmail plot — not his normal line of business — but he's using it to mask his real aim, which is *you*.'

'The blackmail plot you refer to concerning the Shlessinger brother and sister?' Holmes asked, and Lestrade frowned.

'The same. You know about them?' he asked sharply.

'As it happens, I do.'

'Involving 'Gussie' Milverton . . . Charles Augustus of that ilk?'

Holmes nodded. 'The same.'

Lestrade hesitated. 'Look, Mr. Holmes,' he said, slowly. 'I won't ask no more questions. I wouldn't get answers if you didn't want to give them, anyway. You're a private detective, with your client to think of, but I tell you, I mean to get Moran on a blackmail charge and see him put away in Dartmoor for twenty years. Which will put you out of danger for a long time.'

'An exercise on which, you may rest assured, I will be only too happy to cooperate,' Holmes told him.

Lestrade appeared mollified. 'Many thanks, Mr. Holmes. We'll keep in touch, then.'

They shook hands and Lestrade turned to the door. 'And remember me to Dr. Watson.'

'I will, of course,' Holmes murmured.

Just then came the sound of the front door downstairs opening, and the voices of Mrs. Hudson and Dr. Watson drifted up the stairs.

'It's I, Watson,' the doctor called as he ascended the stairs. 'Bit late, I'm afraid, only . . . ' he broke off as he encountered Lestrade in the doorway. 'Oh, hello, Inspector.'

'Afternoon, Doctor,' Lestrade acknowledged. 'And how are you, then?'

'Very well, thank you.'

Lestrade grinned. 'But, of course, you needs to be, don't you? Your stock in trade, to be 'ale and 'earty. Otherwise your patients would take their pains elsewhere.' He gave a chuckle. 'So long, Doctor. 'Bye, Mr. Holmes.' He began to descend the stairs. 'Afternoon, Mrs. H. I'll see meself out.'

'Afternoon, Inspector.' The housekeeper said. 'Goodbye.'

Upstairs Holmes and Watson heard the front door open and close. Watson closed the door to Holmes' room and looked anxiously at his friend.

'What is it, Watson?'

'I'm rather concerned. Lady Frances isn't at her hotel . . . '

Holmes appeared unworried. 'I know. I have made other temporary arrangements.'

'Oh! Is that why Lestrade was here?'

'No, no. Entirely another matter. I've enrolled Lady Frances's help in another plan I'm putting into effect.'

Watson relaxed somewhat. 'Well, I'm thankful she's all right.' He came into the room and sat in his usual armchair.

Holmes regarded him steadily. 'Now, listen carefully. Colonel Moran has made his first move.' He indicated the window.

Watson glanced uneasily at the window. 'What's he up to?'

'He's rented a room in the house opposite.'

Watson gave a start. 'Rented a room?'

Holmes nodded. 'On the third floor . . . it commands a good view.'

Watson frowned. 'Of . . . of this room?'

'Precisely.'

'Was that what Lestrade came to warn you about?' Watson asked.

Holmes nodded. 'Though I already knew. I'd learned it from my own observation . . . and certain enquiries that I made.'

Watson looked uneasily at the window as realization dawned. 'So you'll be in his line of fire? And he'll have that dreadful gun of his.'

'That is what Lestrade came to warn me about,' Holmes affirmed. 'Moran means to exact his revenge for my killing his companion in crime, Moriarty.'

Watson tightened his lips. 'When really it was Moriarty who tried to kill *you*.'

Holmes spread his hands. 'Whatever — but Moran means to extract his revenge.'

'And you're going to give him the chance,' Watson said accusingly.

Holmes shrugged. 'We shall see . . . What Lestrade did tell me is that Moran is behind the Shlessingers' scheme to blackmail Lady Frances.'

Watson looked surprised. 'You mean he's using that in order to reach you?'

'That is what it amounts to,' Holmes

assented. Then he glanced at the door as there came the sound of the front door bell ringing again.

'That'll be Lady Frances, I expect,' Watson said. 'Don't you think, Holmes, she is singularly appealing?'

Holmes smiled faintly. 'I consider her case singularly appealing; especially now that Moran's involved.'

Downstairs, Mrs. Hudson was opening the front door. Watson's surmise about the latest visitor had been incorrect.

'Good afternoon, madam,' Milverton said. 'I believe I'm expected.'

'You're to go on up, sir,' Mrs. Hudson told him.

'Thank you, my dear,' Milverton murmured smoothly, moving towards the stairs.

'It's the gentleman, Mr. Holmes,' Mrs. Hudson called up behind him.

Watson, for once, was completely taken aback. He stared blankly at Holmes as Milverton entered.

Milverton insinuated himself into the room, leaving the door open a few inches behind him.

The visitor was wearing the same suit and overcoat as he had at the Nursing Home. He stretched out his hand to shake hands with Holmes as Watson stared disbelievingly.

'Mr. Sherlock Holmes . . . delighted to meet you,' Milverton murmured suavely.

Holmes ignored Milverton's hand. 'Good afternoon,' he said briefly. He nodded to his friend. 'Dr. Watson.'

'Ah, yes, of course.' Milverton extended a hand to Watson who also pointedly ignored it. Milverton's smile remained intact. 'How d'you do, Doctor?'

'Good afternoon,' Watson said coldly.

'This is Mr. Milverton,' Holmes said.

'Charles Augustus Milverton,' The visitor said smugly. 'Charmed, I'm sure.'

Watson was still staring at Holmes, waiting for an explanation.

Holmes gave it. 'Whom I've persuaded to call to discuss a matter in which we share an interest.'

'Just a quiet business chat,' Milverton murmured.

Holmes reached into his pocket and took out a letter, which he began reading:

' 'Dear Lady Frances Carfax . . . I am in possession of some information concerning yourself and the Honourable Philip Green, about which I can be of help to you. It is of some urgency, so will call this afternoon at three o'clock in the hope you will see me. Yours sincerely, George Tamworth'.' He glanced at Watson and added dryly: 'Mr. Milverton sometimes prefers to be known by an alias.'

Milverton shrugged. 'One's business practice often calls for discretion.'

Holmes regarded him steadily. 'And what was this information, which was a matter of such urgency?'

'Lady Frances,' Milverton explained, 'was engaged to be married to the Honourable Philip Green, a member of the distinguished firm of solicitors, of which her brother, Lord Cecil, is the head. Green, however, had met and fallen in love with Cecilia Shlessinger, who at the time was nursing Lady Frances.'

'Nursing!' Watson burst out scornfully. 'She and her brother were systematically poisoning her, as part of a blackmail plot.'

'My dear sir,' Milverton smiled, 'there is nothing you can tell me about the Shlessingers I haven't made it my business to find out. It's their speciality . . . persuading unsuspecting rich women that they can be cured of some imaginary illness.' He reached into his own pocket and took out a letter, which he handed to Holmes.

Holmes gave Milverton a grim look and began to read the letter aloud: ''My dear . . . If I have given you reason to believe I cherish feelings for you that are more than friendship, I am duly sorry. I feel it is better for us both if we don't meet again . . . ' he broke off. 'I have already read this, of course.'

'Including the postscript?' Milverton pressed.

Holmes looked at the letter again. ''As for the bonds, I intend to hang on to them. No one will know where they are'.' He looked at Milverton. 'How did you come by this?'

'It was given to me.'

'By whom?' Holmes asked sharply.

Milverton pointed to the letter in Holmes' hand. 'Him.'

'Knowing what use you intend to make of it?'

Milverton nodded. 'He wanted £250 for it. We settled for £100.'

'So Philip Green is party to your scheme to blackmail his ex-fiancée?' Holmes asked thoughtfully.

Milverton nodded. 'He'd already absconded with her bonds, so why not pick up a little extra while he was about it?'

Holmes looked at the frowning Watson. 'It makes one wonder, doesn't it, how Lady Frances could have been in love with such a rogue in the first place.'

Watson shook his head. 'It does indeed, Holmes.'

'Some women prefer rogues,' Milverton smirked, 'so I'm told.'

Holmes looked again at the letter. 'I notice it says: 'I have gone away'. And, no doubt, he left no forwarding address.'

Milverton shrugged. 'I wasn't sufficiently interested to ask.'

'Of course,' Watson said acidly, 'your only interest is the saving of Lady Frances's reputation?'

Milverton smiled. 'And her brother's, don't forget. Imagine the damage to Lord Cecil's reputation . . . not to mention his standing in Society . . . if it became known that a member of his firm had, shall we say, jilted his sister and absconded with the loot.'

'And what,' Holmes asked pointedly, 'is the asking price to prevent what you have so graphically described?'

'A mere ten thousand.'

'You scoundrel!' Watson shouted.

Holmes waved a deprecating hand. To Milverton he said: 'In exchange for your copy . . . the only existing copy . . . of this letter?' He indicated Green's first letter.

'That is the deal,' Milverton affirmed.

'Would you, as part of the . . . er . . . 'deal', rack your brains and contrive to recall where Philip Green might be?' Holmes asked pointedly.

Milverton stared at him. 'I can't,' he said slowly. 'I tell you, I don't know.'

'You disappoint me,' Holmes murmured. 'But let us suppose my client, however reluctantly, agrees to your demand, how can you be trusted not to retain another copy of the letter?'

Milverton spread his hands and smiled. 'You must accept my word.'

'The word of a blackmailer!' Dr. Watson snapped angrily.

Holmes smiled enigmatically. 'Tell me, Mr. Milverton, how would you describe yourself? As a brave man, or a rather timid one?'

Milverton looked surprised. 'I . . . I would describe myself simply as a reasonable person, inclined to generosity,' he said slowly.

Holmes turned and crossed to his writing desk, with his back to Milverton. He began to open a drawer in the desk. 'You see, you — a known criminal — came here, unaccompanied . . . '

'At your invitation,' Milverton said.

Still fiddling with the desk drawer, Holmes continued speaking slowly: 'With the object of extracting from Lady Frances Carfax £10,000 in exchange for

a letter written to her by an acknowledged accomplice. Surely, then, all I need
do by way of reply . . . ' Taking a revolver
from the desk drawer, Holmes suddenly
spun round, and aimed it at Milverton.
' . . . is shoot you down like the dog you
are!'

Watson gave a gasp of astonishment.
'Holmes!'

Holmes smiled grimly as Milverton
cringed. 'With Dr. Watson here as witness
that when, on behalf of my client, I
refused your demand, you attacked
me . . . which, of course, I will explain to
Scotland Yard.'

'And I'll back you up, every word!'
Watson vowed.

Milverton was badly scared. 'If . . . if
you did that, my death would be
avenged,' he said, rallying. 'You would be
dead within twenty-four hours.'

'I see . . . so you have accomplices,
other than Green?'

Milverton remained silent for a while,
realizing he had said too much. Then:
'We're talking about you and me, when
it's your client we should be discussing.

Her future happiness and peace of mind are at stake.'

Deadlock. Holmes stared intently at Milverton, who returned the stare, before eventually glancing away. At length Holmes gave a shrug.

'A very persuasive argument.' He returned his revolver to the writing desk drawer, then turned back to Milverton. 'Very well, I will let you have Lady Frances's decision as soon as possible.'

Milverton relaxed a little. 'If you would telephone me tomorrow — you have my number?'

'Yes, I have your number.'

'Say at midday?' At Holmes' nod, Milverton continued: 'And we can arrange a meeting when the transaction can take place, to our mutual satisfaction.'

'You will bring the only other copy of this . . . ' Holmes placed the first letter with the second letter on the table.

'And you will have the cash,' Milverton said flatly.

Holmes nodded. 'If that is my client's wish.' He looked at Watson. 'Will you see

Mr. Milverton finds a cab?'

Watson frowned. 'A cab? Oh, all right.'

'Good afternoon, Mr. Milverton,' Holmes said heavily.

'Good afternoon, sir. Charmed to have made your acquaintance.' Milverton went out, followed by Watson.

After waiting until he heard the two men talking to Mrs. Hudson downstairs, Holmes called out quietly:

'All right. My Lady, you may come out of hiding.'

Lady Frances Carfax emerged from a cupboard. She was dressed in smart, everyday clothes, and was struggling to keep her emotions under control.

'You were marvellous, Mr. Holmes,' she told him.

At that moment Dr. Watson came back into the room, and froze in astonishment. 'Lady Frances! But where have you sprung from?'

Holmes smiled faintly. 'My client and I agreed it would be a good idea for her to know precisely — word for word, in fact, every detail of this attempt to blackmail her.'

Watson came forward and arranged a chair for Lady Frances, but she elected to remain standing. 'You are very brave,' he commented.

Lady Frances tossed her head. 'And, of course, it is all lies . . . horrible lies. Philip's not a thief . . . he's not!'

'Of course not,' Holmes assented. 'Milverton gave us proof of that.' He indicated the two letters he had placed on the table.

'How do you mean?' Lady Frances asked.

'That was one reason for my asking him here,' Holmes explained. 'As I surmised, the letter Philip Green is supposed to have written to you is a forgery.'

Lady Frances clenched her fists. 'Oh, my God . . . that dreadful man!'

'How can you tell that?' Watson asked.

Holmes held out both letters for the others to see. 'Compare the 's' in Milverton's 'Dear Lady Frances'. It's remarkably similar to the 's' in 'sorry' in Green's letter.'

Watson and Lady Frances stared at the

letters, then nodded their heads in agreement.

'Note the 'r' in cherish and friendship is identical with the 'r' in information and afternoon in this.' Holmes went on, indicating the second letter. 'The only differences in the handwriting is that the letter supposed to be from Philip Green was written with an ordinary pen, Milverton's with a fountain pen.'

'He didn't foresee you would read both letters.' Watson pointed out.

Holmes nodded. 'Even the shrewdest of us can't foresee every eventuality.'

'If Philip didn't write that . . . that letter, where is he?' Lady Frances faltered.

'I'm afraid that he's held captive,' Holmes told her gently.

'A prisoner?' Watson regarded Holmes anxiously. 'Who's holding him?'

Lady Frances put her hand to her head and sank into the chair.

Quickly Holmes waved a hand to Watson indicating that he should say nothing more, and turned to the distraught Lady Frances. She looked up at him imploringly.

'But he's alive . . . they haven't . . . ?'

'I'm sure he is in no danger,' Holmes said reassuringly.

'His captors could have no reason to harm him,' Watson added quickly.

'So long as that creature gets his money,' Lady Frances said miserably.

'No, no . . . ' Holmes shook his head. 'He won't.' He leaned down and took hold of Lady Frances's arm. 'Now, you can rest assured that the man you love and who loves you is not the scoundrel he was made out to be.'

'I . . . I never really thought he could be,' she said quietly.

'Now, I want you to return to your hotel,' Holmes said crisply, helping her to get to her feet. 'A cab is waiting for you,' he added, glancing at his watch.

'I'm so grateful to you,' she said, releasing his hand.

'I want you to wait there,' Holmes instructed her, 'until Dr. Watson and I bring Philip Green to you, to tell you, in person, that he's safe.'

'I will see you safely back,' Watson said promptly.

'No, Watson,' Holmes cut in. 'Mrs. Hudson will accompany Lady Frances.'

'Oh!' Watson looked his disappointment.

'Thank you, Mr. Holmes.' Lady Frances turned to go, then noticed Holmes' violin on the writing desk. 'A violin!' She picked it up carefully. 'Do you play?'

'Occasionally, when I have time . . . '

'Oh, how wonderful,' Lady Frances enthused. 'I adore the violin. You must come to my next musical evening. I used to have them regularly and, now I'm better, I shall start again.'

'You're very kind,' Holmes demurred, 'but really I play only for my own amusement.'

'Nonsense, Holmes!' Watson said. 'I think you play very well.'

Holmes moved quickly to door and called downstairs to his landlady. 'Mrs. Hudson! Lady Frances is just leaving.'

'Yes, Mr. Holmes,' she called back. 'The cab is ready, waiting.'

'Thank you, Mrs. Hudson,' Holmes called back. Then he turned to Lady

Frances. 'When you're ready.'

'I'll see you downstairs,' Watson said eagerly.

Lady Frances smiled. 'Thank you, Doctor.'

Holmes stayed at the door as they hurried downstairs. Suddenly the wall-telephone began ringing, and Holmes glanced at his watch. Slowly he went to the telephone, and paused. The phone stopped ringing. Holmes waited. Then the phone started ringing again, After waiting for a few moments, Holmes lifted the phone.

'That you, Billy? Right on time . . . what's your news? Oh, did he? So instead, you dropped him at the corner, I see. Splendid. I will be in touch with your well-earned fee.' Smiling to himself, Holmes hung up.

He turned as Watson re-entered the room.

'I heard you on the telephone as I came up the stairs,' he said. 'Who's Billy?'

'My taxi-driver spy . . . who took Milverton back to where he lives.'

'Ah, yes, of course,' Watson said admiringly. 'You always did have the best underworld contacts . . . as you call them . . . in London.'

'London?' Holmes raised an eyebrow. 'My dear Watson, I have access to the most comprehensive 'grapevine' — to use the vernacular — in all Europe.'

'Yes, yes,' Watson said hurriedly, 'and what did he report?'

'Milverton, as I rather suspected he might, switched the address he first gave to the corner of Tamworth Road, and walked . . . '

' . . . To the Shlessingers' Nursing Home?' Watson asked shrewdly.

Holmes nodded. 'And the hairs at the back of my neck are prickling, Watson.'

'You mean?'

'Moran is using the Shlessingers' attempts at blackmailing Lady Frances to lure me to my destruction . . . correct?'

'I suppose so,' Watson admitted worriedly, 'but how?'

'In his Indian Army days the Colonel's hobby was big game hunting, at which he was renowned. His modus operandi was to tie a young goat to a tree in the vicinity where he knew his quarry hunted its prey, while he waited hidden with his gun.' Holmes tightened his lips. 'That very special gun of his, ready for the kill.'

Watson gave a little shiver. 'And in this case?'

'Philip Green is the prey; I am the quarry.'

Abruptly the phone rang again. Watson started, then smiled apologetically at Holmes, who was making no move to answer the phone.

'Another of your underworld contacts?'

'If you would be kind enough to answer it,' Holmes told him.

'Of course.' Watson hurried to the phone, and was about to answer it, when he turned to Holmes. 'Are you at home?'

Holmes shrugged.

Watson put his hand over the mouth-piece as he listened to the voice at the other end of phone. 'It's that so-called nurse, putting on a voice, asking for me.'

Holmes strode forward quickly and, taking the phone from Watson, said:

'This is Sherlock Holmes speaking. Who is that?'

Cecilia's voice sounded indistinctly.

'No. Dr. Watson's left to visit a patient.'
He paused; there was no reply.

Holmes hung up.

'It *was* her, wasn't it?' Watson asked.
'Why would she want to speak to me?'

Holmes shrugged and smiled faintly.
'She didn't. It was a device to find out if I
am alone.' He turned to look across at the
window.

Watson followed his glance. 'For
Colonel Moran's benefit, of course.' As
Holmes nodded, he added: 'And now he
believes you are alone?'

'Doubtless, he will act.'

Watson watched nervously as Holmes
went to the mantelpiece, taking his pipe
from his pocket. He filled it from the
Persian slipper, taking his time.

Watson shifted his gaze from Holmes to
the window, and back again. He watched
as Holmes lit up, and puffed at his pipe,
blowing smoke towards the window.

Holmes held out his free hand towards
Watson. 'Your hat, Watson,' he requested.

Watson frowned, not understanding the
reason for the odd request. As Holmes
snapped his fingers impatiently, Watson

picked up his hat from where he'd placed it on the back of a chair, and handed it to Holmes.

The detective took a deep drag at his pipe, and as he expelled tobacco-smoke towards the window, he suddenly threw his hat up, also towards the window.

Instantly a pane of glass in the window was shattered by a bullet that smashed into a large vase on the mantelpiece, causing it to crash in several pieces into the fireplace with a startling effect.

'My God!' Watson jumped as if he had been shot.

The bullet lodged in a large book on the mantlepiece, knocking it down into the fireplace. It brought down other books after it, adding to the terror of the shot.

'All right,' Holmes said coolly. 'No harm done.'

As Watson started to go to the window, Holmes halted him.

'Stay where you are, Watson,' he warned. 'You're not here, remember . . . you're visiting a patient.'

Watson was visibly shaken. 'Yes, yes, of

course,' he gasped.

Holmes stooped down to pick the bullet out of the book. 'A rifle bullet designed to explode on impact, inflicting extensive damage,' he murmured, examining it.

'But this is attempted murder. Horrible murder!' Watson said.

Holmes nodded calmly. 'My hope is that Moran feels he's succeeded in his attempt.'

'I ... I don't follow,' Watson said dazedly.

'He believes me to be alone,' Holmes explained crisply, 'so his next step must be to send someone to ascertain if the bullet has found its billet.'

He crossed to the writing desk, opened a drawer, and took out a mask of a shattered, blood-stained face. He placed the mask over his own face, and turned to Watson.

The effect was quite horrific.

'As a doctor, how's this for a human face shattered by that bullet?' he asked sardonically.

'Very realistic.' Watson turned away

with a little shudder.

Holmes smiled behind the hideous mask. 'Splendid! Now, I predict, they'll be over any second to check the damage.'

Even as he finished speaking the front door bell rang downstairs.

Watson was flustered. 'But who'll let them in? Mrs. Hudson's out.'

'Of course,' Holmes murmured. 'That's why I sent her off with Lady Frances.'

Watson stared incredulously at Holmes. 'You mean — you've *planned* all this?'

Holmes handed Watson his revolver, and pushed him towards his bedroom. 'They'll have a skeleton key.'

As Watson closed the bedroom door behind him, Holmes quickly sprawled on floor.

Downstairs the front door opened and there came the sound of footsteps ascending stairs rapidly.

Holmes groaned loudly, as if in agony.

Cecilia's voice sounded outside the door. 'Is anyone there?'

Holmes groaned again. The door opened.

'Mr. Holmes?' Slowly Cecilia entered the room.

'Help me,' Holmes groaned feebly, 'help me . . . '

Cecilia went across to Holmes, and stared down at him with simulated horror. 'Oh, my God, who's done this?'

'Milverton . . . ' Holmes gasped.

'Milverton?'

'I . . . I've put a stop to his blackmail . . . ' Holmes coughed thickly and groaned again. 'Get help quickly . . . or I'm done for.'

Cecilia straightened and turned for the door. 'I'll find help, trust me!' She went out, calling back, 'Quick as I can . . . '

As she went out and hurried down the stairs, Holmes sat up, listening intently. He heard the front door slam shut and scrambled to his feet.

'All right, Watson!' he called out.

Watson came in from the bedroom. 'It worked, Holmes!'

'So far, so good,' Holmes said.

'You think that Moran will come himself to . . . to . . . ?'

'To administer the *coup de grace?*' Holmes nodded. 'He's not going to miss a chance like this. He'll be over in next to no time. So, Watson — '

'Yes . . . yes?'

'Back to your post with gun at the ready,' Holmes instructed, urging Watson back to the bedroom. 'Moran believes me to be alone and at death's door.'

Bending down he sprawled on the floor as before, tensing as he heard the front door opening and slamming.

'Stand by, Watson!' he whispered loudly. As the footsteps sounded outside the door he began groaning and coughing.

'Help . . . help, someone.'

Colonel Moran entered the room cautiously, but with a purposeful tread. He was a big man, wearing an expensive suit. Hatless, he carried his 'gun-stick' over his left arm.

Crossing quickly to Holmes, he stood staring down at him with a triumphant expression.

'So . . . Sherlock Holmes, we meet again!'

'Help me,' Holmes groaned from where he still lay on the floor, apparently not seeing Moran.

Moran grinned crookedly. 'Oh, I'll help you . . . ' He prodded Holmes with his foot. 'It's Moran . . . here to send you to join Moriarty!'

Holmes raised himself slightly, as if realizing for the first time who was addressing him. 'Moran! *You!*'

Moran aimed his gun-stick at Holmes, then changed his mind, looking about him. 'But, no . . . I won't waste another bullet on you.'

He reached out a hand and took a cushion from the nearest chair.

'This will put a stop to your groaning!' he said viciously, and bent down, intent on suffocating Holmes with the cushion.

Instantly Holmes reached up and dragged him down, at the same time getting to his feet, and reversing the situation.

He held Moran tightly in a ju-jitsu grip, and called out urgently:

'Watson!'

Watson came rushing in from the bedroom, revolver levelled at Moran. 'All right, Moran!' he snapped.

'Get up,' Holmes told Moran, releasing

him from his grip. 'We won't shoot you down, like a dog.'

He pulled off the mask and threw it on the table.

'Put your hands up and keep them up!' Watson waved the revolver at Moran, who got slowly to his feet and raised his hands.

Holmes stooped and picked up the gun-stick, and hooked it over his own arm.

Moran instinctively lowered his hands, attempting to reach for his gun. 'That's mine!' he snarled.

'Keep your hands up!' Watson warned sharply. 'Or I'll . . . '

Moran spun to face Watson, arms wide apart, as if daring him to shoot.

'Dr. Watson . . . surely not? When your sole purpose for existence on this troubled planet is to save life . . . not destroy it.'

Watson's expression betrayed that the words had clearly disturbed him, and he turned to Holmes for guidance.

The detective did not answer, his attention remaining fixed on Moran, who now turned to him and spoke softly:

'While, at the same time, I'm sure, you can explain to your bloodthirsty friend, what will surely happen, should he carry out his homicidal threat?'

Holmes tightened his lips with sick realization. 'You have left explicit instructions that the innocent person you hold captive will be summarily dealt with.'

'Philip Green!' Watson gasped. He lowered the revolver and turned to Holmes.

'So the message has got through,' Moran laughed grimly. 'You have lost the day, Holmes.'

'Not the day; only this round.'

Moran visibly relaxed. 'You know, your lack of comprehension of the facts almost amuses me. You will never win. I *shall* avenge Moriarty . . . ' He began backing to the door. 'So be warned, Holmes. And,' he pointed to the gun-stick, 'I'll have *that* back, I swear it.'

After the door slammed, Watson rushed towards it, and shouted after Moran. 'You murderous swine!'

Moments later the front door downstairs slammed shut.

'Save your breath, Watson,' Holmes told him. The doctor turned back to his friend dejectedly.

Holmes took back his revolver, and returned it to the writing desk.

'What can we do?' Watson asked, as Holmes calmly produced his pipe, refilling it, and lighting up.

Watson slumped dejectedly into a chair, his eyes on Holmes.

'First,' Holmes mused, 'let us count our blessings, so to speak. See what I have achieved in my client's interests, since taking on the case this morning.' He looked at Watson sharply. 'Only this morning, d'you realize that?'

'Of course, you've done splendidly.' Watson's dejection belied his words.

Holmes smiled faintly. 'Ah, I beg your pardon, I should have phrased that more generously ... it is what *we* have achieved, my dear Watson.'

Watson perked slightly. 'Oh, I did nothing. I simply followed your instructions.'

Holmes clapped him on the shoulder. 'No, you acted with determination and the highest courage.'

'Oh, my dear chap, really!'

'We have rescued Lady Frances from the clutches of the Shlessingers,' Holmes went on incisively, 'and, at the same time, totally destroyed Milverton's vile scheme to blackmail her . . . ' He broke off at the sound of the front door opening downstairs.

The voice of Mrs. Hudson called up to them. 'I'm back, Mr. Holmes.'

Holmes crossed to door, and called down to his housekeeper. 'Thank you, Mrs. Hudson.'

'I left the lady safe and well,' she called up to him.

'Splendid,' Holmes said approvingly. 'And now, could you do something else, please?'

'I know what you're going to say,' Mrs. Hudson chuckled. 'Bring you and Dr. Watson a fresh pot of tea.'

'You are worthy of stardom as a mind reader on the music halls, Mrs. Hudson,' Holmes called down.

'Oh, Mr. Holmes!' Mrs. Hudson bustled off to her kitchen

'Tea, Holmes!' Watson expostulated. 'But surely we should be planning our next move!'

'We are,' Holmes spoke calmly. 'We're regrouping our resources to mount another — this time successful — attack.'

Watson let out a sigh, relaxing. 'Oh. Yes, well, perhaps a cup of tea is a good idea.'

Holmes relit his pipe, which had gone out. 'One hazard we hadn't foreseen was Philip Green's involvement.'

Watson gave a start. 'Heavens, yes. If anything should happen to him — '

'But, even in his case, we may feel encouraged.'

'Yes, we know where they've got him,' Watson said. 'Unless they decide to move him.'

Holmes shook his head. 'We've given Moran no reason to suspect what we know and shifting Green to yet another hiding place today would present difficulties.'

The voice of Mrs. Hudson sounded cheerily: 'Tea on its way, Mr. Holmes!'

'Splendid!' Holmes went across to the table and cleared away the mask into the writing table drawer.

Mrs. Hudson entered with a tray with tea-things, and quickly placed the items on the table, Watson assisting.

'There we are, then,' Mrs. Hudson said. 'Just what the Doctor ordered! Eh, Dr. Watson?' she added archly, putting a plate of biscuits on the table. 'And some of those biscuits I know you specially like.'

'Thank you, Mrs. Hudson,' Watson smiled.

After checking everything was in order. Mrs. Hudson turned and went out with the empty tray.

'Thank you, Mrs. Hudson,' Holmes called after her, knocking his pipe out into an ashtray and returning it to his pocket.

For a moment they drank their tea appreciatively, Watson nibbling a biscuit, Holmes pacing up and down as he drank his tea, his brow wrinkled in concentrated thought. Suddenly he stopped his pacing. 'That's it!'

'What is?' Watson looked up.

'My reference to Mrs. Hudson performing on the music halls . . . her cousin, stage door keeper at the Holborn Empire, was brutally robbed by a thug named Benskin. I got him five years.'

Watson looked his puzzlement. 'A criminal named Benskin who robbed Mrs. Hudson's cousin? My dear Holmes, what on earth has that to do with our problem?'

'He'd been employed as a temporary barman at the public house nearby called The Limping Man,' Holmes explained. 'Coincidentally, he was crippled in his right leg . . . and left behind a blood-stained footprint, which I was able to prove was his.'

Watson was still puzzled. 'I still don't see the relevance to Colonel Moran and . . .'

'He shouted from the dock that he'd 'get me' for putting him away.' Holmes spun and pointed to the writing desk. 'Watson . . . in the second drawer down you'll find my theatrical makeup.'

Watson stared at Holmes as if he'd taken leave of his senses. 'Theatrical makeup?'

Holmes crossed quickly to the wall-phone and dialled a number. Watson stood dithering, still not knowing what to make of Holmes' instructions. His puzzlement increased when Holmes added, over his shoulder: 'And also a hand mirror.'

'A hand mirror!' Watson muttered to himself.

Holmes spoke into the telephone: 'Billy? Holmes here. A cab straight away. To the corner of Tamworth Road.'

Watson turned in surprise. 'Tamworth Road?'

Holmes hurried past him, into the bedroom. 'Benskin was of much the same height and build as myself and, with the aid of makeup, I aim to impersonate him.'

Watson was now completely nonplussed. 'Impersonate — you mean . . . ?'

'I'll need spirit-gum and some crêpe hair,' Holmes told him, calling from the bedroom.

'You mean, you're going to the Shlessingers, disguised as . . . ?'

Holmes called through again from the bedroom. 'In the bookshelf you'll see my rogues' gallery file . . . you'll find Benskin's photo.'

Watson went into action promptly, and

soon found sticks of makeup, and spirit-gum from a drawer, along with a false moustache and crêpe hair, which he brought to the table, pushing aside the tea-things. He found a hand mirror, which he placed on the table, and then the file in the bookcase. Opening it, he began checking the photos.

Holmes continued talking from the bedroom. 'I've got some apparel appropriate for the rôle . . . the sort Benskin will be wearing . . . he'll be just out of prison . . . '

A moment later Holmes appeared dramatically at the bedroom door. 'What d'you think, Watson?'

He was wearing a shabby suit with a cap stuffed in a pocket; a skullcap drawn over his head gave it the appearance of being close-shaven. Oddest of all was the fact that his right leg appeared shorter than the other.

Watson stared at him in utter disbelief and dropped the photo-file.

'Good God! Is it you, Holmes?'

Holmes advanced into the room, limping slightly, his face contorted in an evil grimace. Several of his teeth appeared to be missing, and when he answered Watson he did so in a Cockney accent.

'Yus, I've heard it over the grapevine, Colonel Moran, as you're out to get Sherlock Bloody Holmes . . . 'im wot got me sent down for five for a crime I never done . . . I'm your man, Colonel, to help you fix the bastard good and proper!'

Watson straightened from picking up the dropped file. 'It's absolutely marvellous, Holmes!'

'Now, I just need to add some touches,' Holmes went on urgently, seating himself at the table.

He instructed Watson to put the photo-file on the table, and searched through it to find the photo he wanted. At length he gave a grunt of satisfaction.

'Here he is . . . Arthur Benskin full face and profile.' He placed the photo so he could copy from it, and deftly started to apply make-up, while Watson held the mirror for him.

'A touch of prison-pallor, I think will be suitable,' Holmes murmured. 'And, now that drooping moustache . . . they'd let him keep that, since it's in his mug-shots, as they're described in prison slang.'

After his initial enthusiasm for Holmes' disguise, Watson began to have doubts.

'But . . . but you'll be putting your head in the lion's mouth.'

'Not *my* head,' Holmes said dryly. 'Benskin's! Spirit-gum, please.'

Watson handed him a brush with gum on it, which Holmes applied to his upper lip. 'That moustache will do the trick, I think,' Holmes muttered. He took a false moustache from Watson and applied it to his upper lip, dabbing it on carefully with a large handkerchief.

The front door rang downstairs. Holmes turned and shouted downstairs:

'That'll be Billy, Mrs. Hudson. Tell him I'm in a hurry.'

'Yes, Mr. Holmes, I'll tell him,' Mrs. Hudson called back.

'Mr. Holmes won't be a minute, Billy,' she informed the caller after opening the door to him, 'and he'll be in a hurry.' She thought to herself: 'Though I must say

I've never known him when he wasn't.'

Upstairs Holmes moved to his writing desk and from a drawer extracted a hypodermic needle and phial.

'Holmes!' Watson cried, horrified. 'No!'

Ignoring Watson's imprecations, Holmes rolled up his sleeve, expertly filled hypodermic from phial and injected his forearm.

'You swore you would give it up!' Watson said accusingly.

Holmes rolled down his sleeve and returned the hypodermic and phial to the drawer. Closing it, he turned to his agitated friend.

'Do not concern yourself, Watson, I'm no Dr. Jekyll about to turn himself into a Mr. Hyde! I'm merely stimulating my histrionic powers, to give the rôle I'm about to play its fullest effect.' With that he strode out of the room.

'God bless you, Holmes,' Watson muttered, shaking his head.

At the foot of the stairs Holmes encountered Mrs. Hudson.

'I shan't be long, Mrs. Hudson,' he told her.

'Oh, Mr. Holmes! I hardly recognized you!'

Their voices carried faintly upstairs to Watson. As he heard the front door close, he turned back to the table; then suddenly remembering something, he went across to the desk drawer.

Pulling out Holmes' revolver, he dashed to the top of the stairs and shouted down:

'Holmes! Your revolver! You've forgotten it. You've forgotten your revolver!'

3

A storm was breaking over London. Intermittent flashes of lightning were followed by rumbles of thunder. In his laboratory at the Nursing Home Dr. Shlessinger was busy in his laboratory, handling a phial and a hypodermic syringe.

A lightning flash made him aware of the gathering darkness, and he paused in his work to switch on the laboratory light.

The light spilled through the open laboratory door into the adjacent darkened room. There came a further rumble of thunder and a distant lightning flash.

Shlessinger fingered his collar. 'Phew . . . it's damned warm,' he muttered.

Coming out of the laboratory he crossed to the French windows, and opened one of them to let in some fresh air.

The front door bell was ringing, but a further rumble of thunder prevented

Shlessinger from hearing it as he returned to his laboratory, and continued his dealings with the phial and syringe.

As the front door bell continued to ring again, more insistently, he abruptly became aware of it.

As he turned quickly to come out of the laboratory, he dropped the phial.

'Damn and blast!' he muttered, stooping to retrieve the phial.

As the front door bell continued to ring loud and long he shouted out: 'All right! I hear you!'

Quickly picking up phial he replaced it with the syringe on a laboratory bench, and hurried out of the laboratory, as the bell continued ringing.

Hurrying into the hall he shouted again: 'I heard you, I tell you!'

Yanking open the front door he found Milverton glaring at him.

'What the devil's happening?' Milverton demanded impatiently. 'I've been ringing for hours!'

'All right . . . all right,' Shlessinger grumbled. 'I was in the lab and I couldn't hear you for the thunder.' As they crossed the hall, he switched on the lights.

Milverton looked about him. 'Where's the Colonel?'

'He's not back yet. Why, anything he needs to know?'

Milverton nodded. 'He'll want to hear about my meeting with Holmes.'

'So — how did it go?'

Before Milverton could answer there sounded a muffled cry from the direction of the hall.

'Help . . . help me, *help me*, someone . . . ' It was Philip Green, crying for help.

Milverton gave a start. 'Who the devil's that?'

Shlessinger looked towards the door and shrugged. 'It's Philip Green . . . I'm just going to give him another jab.'

The French window suddenly slammed together with a bang; causing both men to jump. Quickly Shlessinger crossed the room and closed them, turning the key in the lock. 'The thunder made it a bit warm in here,' he explained.

Green's voice sounded again. 'Help . . . help me . . . *oh, help* . . . '

Milverton looked down at the syringe Shlessinger was now holding. 'That the same stuff you used on Lady Frances?'

'No, it's something I'm experimenting with,' Shlessinger said, going to the doorway into the hall.

Milverton gave a little shudder. 'Gives me the creeps, that does.'

Shlessinger looked at him cynically. 'Bit squeamish, aren't we?'

'Perhaps, but . . . '

Shlessinger snorted. 'Coming from you . . . a murderer of souls . . . as Justice Wade described one of your lot the other day, giving him ten years!'

Milverton shrugged and remained standing at the door, watching as Shlessinger crossed to one of several doors that led off from the hall and opened it.

Green screamed at him. 'Help . . . ' he broke off, as he saw the syringe. 'No . . . no . . . leave me alone . . . leave me alone!'

Deliberately, Shlessinger closed the door.

As he saw the closing door, the watching Milverton turned away from the doorway, and went back into the room. He took a cigarette from his case, and nervously operated his lighter.

'Perhaps I am getting squeamish,' he muttered to himself. 'Murderer of the soul! What nonsense . . . '

He stood staring into the laboratory as he drew on the cigarette, then turned expectantly as a door slammed.

Shlessinger came back into the room from the hall, still carrying the syringe. 'That's taken care of him . . . for the time being!'

Shlessinger turned into his laboratory and laid the syringe on a bench. Switching off the laboratory light, he rejoined Milverton, closing the door behind him.

'Pretty strong stuff, eh?' Milverton commented, aware that Green had ceased his moaning.

Shlessinger nodded. 'You have to be careful not to overdo it.'

'If you did,' Milverton asked curiously, 'would it leave any signs?'

'It wouldn't show in the blood . . . but you'd have to explain the needle marks!'

Milverton glanced towards the hall door. 'How long can you keep him . . . quiet?'

Shlessinger shrugged. 'As long as the Colonel requires. By the way, how *did* it go with Sherlock Holmes?'

'Oh, I'm to collect tomorrow, in return for Green's letter — so-called.'

'The £10,000?'

'No cash, no deal.' Milverton's tone changed. 'That's what you expected me to say, isn't it?'

'Well . . . isn't that what he wanted to talk to you about?' Shlessinger asked.

'And you think I fell for it?' Milverton snapped.

Shlessinger looked surprised by his tone. 'What . . . what you getting at?'

'It was just a trap,' Milverton told him briefly.

'A trap . . . what do you mean?'

Milverton tightened his lips. 'Put yourself in Holmes' shoes. He has a good idea that the letter is a fake, neither does he believe Green took off with the bonds.'

'What are you telling me?' Shlessinger asked deliberately.

A flicker of lightning, and a distant

rumble of thunder caused Milverton to glance at the French windows, as Shlessinger frowned to assimilate what he'd been told.

'It was a trap, set to lure the Colonel, of course,' Milverton said briefly.

Shlessinger nodded slowly. 'You mean, Holmes knows he's got to get Moran before Moran gets him?'

'That's it. And he's guessed the Colonel's using Philip Green as bait to trap him. At the same time, he's got to rescue Green, to earn his fee from this Lady Frances.'

'So that's why Moran's transferred Green here?'

Milverton nodded. 'And why Holmes had me followed from Baker Street.'

Shlessinger gave a start. 'What?

'The cab I took just 'happened to be passing' . . . which was a trifle too convenient, I thought,' Milverton said.

'So you neatly switched to another one, of course?'

Milverton smiled. 'Better than that. I got out and walked . . . ' he paused as there came the sound of the front door opening and shutting.

Cecilia's voice sounded from the hall. 'Anyone home?' A moment later she came into the room. 'Where's Moran?'

'Why?' her brother asked. 'What's the news?'

She gave a mirthless smile. 'Only that I left him with Sherlock Holmes . . . settling his fate, once and for all.'

Shlessinger frowned. 'What?

'Yes, what d'you mean?' Milverton demanded.

'I've just told you,' Cecilia explained calmly. 'Sherlock Holmes is dead! Finished . . . done for!'

'Who killed him?' Milverton asked sharply.

'Ask Colonel Moran!'

'He did it?' Shlessinger gripped his sister's arm.

Cecilia nodded, quite unmoved. 'He used his gun-stick, from the house opposite, then sent me over to check.'

Shlessinger exhaled slowly. 'Sherlock Holmes put out of business forever . . . '

'I saw him lying there with my own eyes, his face shattered,' Cecilia affirmed.

She gave a little shudder. 'He wasn't a pretty sight, I can tell you. He begged me to help him.'

Shlessinger smiled. 'It's the most wonderful news . . . '

'I could have finished him off myself,' Cecilia told him, 'only I daren't rob the Colonel of the pleasure!'

'So,' Milverton mused, stubbing out his cigarette in an ashtray, 'the great Sherlock Holmes is no more.'

Shlessinger looked at his sister. 'How is this going to affect our plans?'

Cecilia shrugged. 'It can't be anything else but to the good.' She turned to Milverton, 'What's *your* news?'

'Putting the black on Lady Frances isn't going to work,' Shlessinger cut in before Milverton could answer.

'What d'you mean?' Cecilia demanded angrily.

'Holmes was too smart for me,' Milverton admitted. 'As I was explaining, what he was after was to get me to reveal Green's hiding place.'

'You didn't?'

'Of course not,' Shlessinger said.

Milverton frowned. 'So, we're left with Green on our hands?'

Shlessinger grunted. 'Well, we can fix that.'

'We'd better wait to see what Colonel Moran thinks,' Milverton said.

'What *I* think,' said Cecilia viciously, 'is that we should give him the same treatment Holmes got. If he escaped, we'd be for it.'

Milverton spread his hands, looking at Shlessinger. 'How can he escape? He's doped all the time.'

'Keeping him here's too risky, I tell you,' Cecilia snapped.

Abruptly an anguished voice was heard just outside the door.

'Help me, someone! *Help me!*'

'What the hell . . . ?' Shlessinger gasped as Green staggered in from the hall, shouting for help. He was utterly dishevelled, wearing trousers and shirt with canvas shoes and was clearly hysterical.

'Help me get out of here!'

Shlessinger and Cecilia grabbed him roughly. 'Shut up, blast you!' Shlessinger snarled.

'I thought you were supposed to keep him quiet?' Cecilia said accusingly.

'I gave him a good jab.'

'Let me go,' Green moaned. 'Let me out of here — '

His voice snapped off as Shlessinger slapped him heavily across the mouth. Immediately a trickle of blood appeared.

'Shut up . . . shut up!' Shlessinger hit him again.

Green sagged, almost knocked out,

'Quick,' Shlessinger told Milverton as he stood gaping. 'Give me a hand.'

Milverton helped Shlessinger support Green, as Cecilia spun towards the laboratory.

'I'll soon fix him up,' she muttered.

'What are you doing?' Shlessinger demanded.

Cecilia's voice sounded from inside the laboratory. 'I'll show you.'

'Not that stuff!' Shlessinger shouted. 'It's deadly!'

Cecilia emerged from the laboratory, with a hypodermic syringe in her hand, obviously intent on drugging Green. '*This'll* keep him quiet,' she asserted viciously.

'Don't do it!' Milverton was thoroughly alarmed. 'You'll kill him!'

Green resumed his moaning. 'Help . . . help . . . get me away from here . . .'

'Shut up, damn you!' Cecilia pushed up the sleeve of Green's left arm, preparing to give him a jab.

'Don't let her!' Green screamed. 'Don't let her do it!'

'Stop it, I tell you,' Shlessinger warned.

There came a sudden flash of lightning, then a roll of thunder — and the lights went out, plunging the room into darkness.

'What the hell?' Shlessinger gasped.

'For God's sake . . . what's going on?' Milverton demanded.

'It's only the storm,' Cecilia said scornfully.

The lights came up again slowly to reveal a tall figure standing in the doorway.

'Colonel Moran!' Shlessinger gasped.

Cecilia and Milverton turned to Moran, then Cecilia moved towards Moran, leaving Milverton struggling to support the semi-collapsed Green.

Moran came slowly into room and held out a hand to Cecilia. The woman hesitated, then handed over the hypodermic to Moran.

He dropped the syringe onto the floor, and stamped his boot on it.

'Get him back to his room,' Moran growled at Milverton. Then he fixed Cecilia with a stare. 'It seems that the female of the species is more deadly than the male!'

Breathing hard, Milverton dragged Green from the room.

Cecilia bent as if to pick up the broken syringe, only for Moran to step in and kick it aside with his right foot. She gave him a bitter look and turned away.

'We didn't hear you, Colonel,' Shlessinger said uncertainly.

'I habitually close doors quietly,' Moran said. He glared at Cecilia. 'Did I order anything in the medical line?'

'It was only intended to quiet him,' Cecilia said sullenly.

Shlessinger spoke enthusiastically, seeking to change the smouldering atmosphere.

'Well, well, Colonel! So, we've got Sherlock Holmes out of our system, eh?'

'I was telling them how you dealt with him,' Cecilia put in quickly.

Milverton came back into the room, wiping his brow with a handkerchief. 'He's out like a light, but I locked the door.'

Moran nodded, then turned to Cecilia. 'I'm afraid Mr. Holmes is still with us.'

Shlessinger's haw dropped. 'What? He's alive?'

Cecilia was incredulous. 'But I saw him . . . all that blood . . . '

'Holmes is very much alive,' Moran said deliberately, looking at Shlessinger.

'You mean it was all a put up job?'

Moran nodded. 'Which explains why I don't want Green to come to any harm.'

'You can use him . . . against Holmes?' Milverton asked shrewdly.

'I believe that opportunity will come my way,' Moran assented.

Shlessinger wrinkled his brow. 'In return for sending him back, you mean?'

Moran nodded. 'I fancy Holmes would feel obliged to return my gun.'

'But surely Green will go straight to the police?' Cecilia protested.

Moran shrugged. 'We can't hold him forever.'

'That's why if we killed him off . . . ' Cecilia began, but Moran cut her off.

'There wouldn't be a corner of the earth where you could hide,' he stated.

'My God, you're right,' Milverton said.

'I must admit, I wouldn't care for the nine o'clock jump either!' Shlessinger said uneasily.

Cecilia turned away, disgusted at the other's timidity.

'It's the second time he's supposed to have been killed,' Moran mused. 'Over the Reichenbach Falls before. Then, today, in his own home, but next time it's going to be third time unlucky for you, Sherlock Holmes!'

Suddenly the front door bell began to ring stridently.

'Who the devil's that?' Shlessinger demanded, startled.

All those in the room became alert and tense, staring at the doorway and hall beyond.

Cecilia glanced at Moran. 'Are you expecting anyone?'

Moran shook his head.

Shlessinger looked suspiciously at Milverton. 'Sure you weren't followed?'

'I'm certain I wasn't.'

The front door bell rang again.

Shlessinger looked worried. 'If it's the police, and they find Green . . . '

'I *said* we should kill him!' Cecilia snapped.

'If it's the police,' Milverton said, thinking, 'and it's him they're after, they'll have a search-warrant.'

The front door bell rang again.

'I'll answer it,' Cecilia decided. She turned to do so, but pulled up with a gasp as Sherlock Holmes — heavily disguised as Benskin — appeared suddenly in the doorway.

'You all deaf?' Holmes asked dryly, his voice disguised. 'I bin ringin' all night.'

'Who the devil are you?' Shlessinger demanded.

'Well, I ain't the Devil . . . that's for starters.'

way. You thought you'd settled Holmes' hash good and proper, only to find he'd turned the tables on you.'

They all stared at Holmes for a long moment, then Moran said slowly:

'I'm sure you have reason to rely on your source of information?'

Holmes smiled. 'None better than my own eyes and ears, Colonel. Next door to 221B Baker Street is number 223 — which lets accommodation at reasonable rates — and where yours truly has had a room since I came out. And my landlady, Ma Griffen, and his Mrs. Hudson, well . . . they has a gossip, now and then. And I listens, and I keeps my peepers peeled about the comings and goings between this house and . . . well . . . '

'Do go on,' Shlessinger invited, his eyes narrowed with interest. 'Surely, there's more to come?'

'Well, yes . . . I gets the word — over the 'grapevine', of course — which is that the Colonel and Sherlock Holmes have clashed . . . and I thinks, well, there might be some pickings in this for yours truly, and calls on His Nibs . . . '

'On Sherlock Holmes himself,' Milverton said wonderingly.

'When was this?' Cecilia asked sharply.

'Soon after you'd left . . . ' Holmes looked at Moran, waiting for him to make some reply, then resumed as Moran remained silent, ' . . . without that special stick of yours, wasn't it, Colonel?'

The others stared at Moran, who tensed, then turned away, taking a few paces before turning back to face Holmes, his face bitter.

'*He* sent you,' he rasped.

Holmes nodded calmly. 'You can 'ave it back . . . in return for your prisoner.'

Again there was a distant flash of lightning, and rumble of thunder fading into distance as Shlessinger glanced out of the French windows.

'The storm's receding,' he commented.

Abruptly the distressed cries from Green resumed. Moran eyed Holmes for a long moment, then turned in the direction of Green's cries.

'Let me out . . . help me, some one . . . *help me* . . . '

'Fetch him,' Moran instructed Milverton.

Milverton nodded hastily, and went out.

Shlessinger looked at Moran. 'It's all a bit of a coincidence, isn't it? Him meeting Holmes the way he says?'

'It's cooked up by Holmes and him . . . Or he's made it all up himself,' Cecilia said sourly.

'That's right . . . chat among yourselves,' Holmes murmured amiably.

Moran made no reply and turned away. Holmes' glance followed him. Moran stayed silent as Green was heard in the hall.

'You can't keep me a prisoner . . . you *can't*, I tell you.'

Green, followed by Milverton, entered from the hall. Milverton was holding Green by his left arm. The hapless prisoner appeared shaken and broken, blood trickling from his mouth.

Moran gave Milverton his pocket handkerchief. 'Clean him up.'

Milverton dabbed Green's face with the handkerchief, as he continued to mutter. 'Let me go . . . let me go free . . . '

'Keep quiet, and listen!' Moran growled at him. He turned to Holmes. 'You're confident Holmes will make the exchange?'

Holmes shrugged. 'You know him better than I do . . . '

Moran scowled thoughtfully. 'He's always been a man of his word, that's true.'

'But you're going to trust *his* word!' Cecilia burst out angrily, pointing at Holmes. 'A damned jailbird!'

'Mind you don't end up one yourself.' Holmes gave her a sardonic smile.

Moran ignored Cecilia's outburst, and looked at Holmes. 'What's *your* reward for all this?'

'Yes, you're not doing this for nothing, I'll bet,' Shlessinger said.

Holmes regarded Moran levelly. 'I'm sure you can be reasonably generous, Colonel, when you want.'

'What's Holmes paying you?' Shlessinger demanded impatiently.

Holmes smiled faintly. 'Not as much as I expect.'

Milverton frowned at Moran. 'Forgive me interrupting . . . but what's to prevent our friend here going straight to the police?'

'That's right,' Cecilia agreed. 'He can have us put away for years!'

Green had been struggling to follow the conversations, the import of which he was now just beginning to understand. 'Of course I won't,' he implored Moran. 'All I want is to get away from here . . . I promise you.'

Moran looked at him. 'I've no alternative but to trust you.'

'I swear I'll keep my word!' Green said desperately.

'You had better do that, if you want to keep your life,' Moran said harshly.

'Holmes will see he doesn't open his mouth,' 'Benskin' put in. 'You said yourself he's a man of his word . . . '

'So long as his . . . er . . . client is happy,' Shlessinger said.

Moran appeared to make up his mind. 'You'll pick up a cab soon enough,' he told Holmes. He glanced at his watch. 'And be at Baker Street in half-an-hour

. . . then back here within the hour.'

Holmes nodded assent. 'With a present for you from His Nibs, which reminds me . . . what's my present to be, Colonel?'

'£100. In two fifty-pound notes.'

'Make it £150, in three fifties . . . and one in advance.'

Moran eyed Holmes for a moment, then reached for his note case. Taking out a £50 note, he handed it to Holmes without speaking.

Holmes took the note eagerly, spat on it, and pocketed it quickly. He turned to Green.

'What are we waiting for, then? Come on.' Grabbing Green by the arm, and urged him out of the room. Pausing in the doorway, he glanced back at Moran. 'See you in an hour . . . with the goods.' Pushing Green ahead of him, he went out and into the hall.

Moran stared after 'Benskin' and Green, his expression enigmatic. Cecilia crossed to doorway and stood watching them out of the front door.

As the front door slammed behind the two men, Milverton looked at Moran uneasily. 'Well, is that it, Colonel?'

'It doesn't mean the cessation of hostilities between me and Holmes, if that's what you're thinking,' Moran replied harshly.

Shlessinger and his sister both looked at Moran sharply.

Milverton looked uncomfortable. 'No, no. It's just that I don't see that there's any part in it for me . . . '

Moran looked at him with faint contempt. 'You'll be finding other fish to fry, eh?'

Milverton nodded eagerly. 'That's right. So, I'll be running along, then.' He crossed to the door. '*Au revoir*, everyone.'

He hurried out.

Moran turned to Cecilia. 'Give him a few minutes; then, just in case he takes a wrong turning and ends up at Scotland Yard, follow him.'

'You can count on me,' Cecilia said, nodding.

Moran looked towards the door and smiled twistedly. Abruptly he called out: 'And as for you, Benskin, you can take a bow for a performance to match any actor on the London stage!'

Shlessinger and Cecilia stared at him in amazement.

'What d'you mean?' Sjlessinger asked

'Just that he was no more Benskin, the burglar, than I am Jack the Ripper . . . that was Sherlock Holmes himself!'

The Shlessingers looked at Moran open-mouthed, dumbfounded.

4

It was early evening on the same day as Sherlock Holmes had engineered his audacious rescue of Philip Green from the Nursing Home.

In his rooms at 221B Baker Street, Colonel Moran's gun-stick lay placed prominently on Holmes' writing desk. In the room also were Dr. Watson and Lady Frances Carfax, both of whom were looking towards the adjoining bedroom door, which stood open.

Lady Frances looked very beautiful and excited as Holmes entered from the bedroom and crossed to join them.

'My razor all right, Mr. Green?' Holmes called back into the bedroom.

'Excellent. You've been most kind, a thousand thanks.'

'We must have you looking your best for Lady Frances's sake,' Holmes smiled, looking at Green's fiancée.

'I'm sure she's most impatient to see

you,' Watson added, his eyes twinkling.

'No more impatient than I am to see her.' Lady Frances' eyes gleamed as she heard Green's voice from the bedroom. 'And thanks, too, for lending me your raincoat.' Green came into the room, buttoning the raincoat up. He stopped in pleased amazement as he saw the girl coming forward to meet him.

'So impatient, my dear Philip that I'm here to meet you!'

Holmes and Watson stepped aside, as Lady Frances and Green embraced each other.

'Frances! Oh, this is wonderful of you!' Watson looked on, immensely pleased, whilst Holmes gave the scene a nod of approval.

Lady Frances gently broke free of his embrace. 'You must thank Mr. Holmes and Dr. Watson for conspiring with me, so we could meet like this.'

'It was simply wonderful of you,' Green told Holmes sincerely. 'And you, too, Doctor.'

'I'm glad it's been such a happy outcome for you,' Holmes commented.

'And we wish you all happiness,' Watson smiled. He glanced in surprise towards the window as from the street below sounded a barrel organ, playing a popular romantic song.

Green laughed. 'Listen, Frances. All Baker Street knows we're happy.'

'Very romantic!' Watson commented dryly, glancing at Holmes.

Lady Frances, with her arm in Green's turned to listen to the barrel organ.

'Wonderful!' she smiled.

'Absolutely marvellous!' Green looked at the faintly smiling Holmes. 'I wouldn't mind betting you arranged it!'

Still smiling enigmatically Holmes joined Watson in following Lady Frances and Green out of room.

Holmes called down to Mrs. Hudson.

'Lady Frances and Mr. Green are leaving, Mrs. Hudson.'

'Yes, Mr. Holmes.'

As Watson and Holmes returned to the room they heard Lady Frances and Green taking their leave of Mrs. Hudson. 'Thank you for all your help,' Lady Frances told the housekeeper, kissing her lightly on the cheek.

'You looks lovely, Lady Frances,' Mrs. Hudson told her, as she opened the front door.

As the front door closed, the barrel organ stopped playing. Inside the room Watson glanced at the window, and turned to Holmes.

'The music's stopped.' Watson narrowed his eyes. 'I do believe you did arrange it.' Holmes shrugged slightly and smiled. 'Oh, Holmes . . . that was a charming thought . . . ' he broke off, suddenly becoming serious. 'Or — was it something to do with — with Colonel Moran?'

'Police agents need to be versatile, artistic, poetical, musical . . . ' Holmes murmured,

'And that was one of them keeping an eye on things?'

Holmes shrugged again. 'We're up against a very resourceful criminal.'

'Then you actually expect a visit from Moran, in an attempt to get this thing back?' Watson moved to pick up the stick-gun.

'It's still loaded,' Holmes warned him. Watson hastily put down the gun-stick.

'And when will he show his hand? This evening?'

'For him,' Holmes answered gravely, 'any other time except this evening will be too late.'

'But, of course, you'll refuse to hand it over?'

Holmes shook his head. 'I doubt very much I'll be given the opportunity to refuse or otherwise.'

'My dear fellow!' Watson was thoroughly alarmed. 'What are you doing to defend yourself? I mean, you're in danger!'

Holmes nodded towards the window. 'I've already had a word with Lestrade.'

'Lestrade? You've called in Scotland Yard?'

'Certainly I have,' Holmes explained. 'After all, it's a kind of criminal conspiracy, involving Milverton and the Shlessingers.'

'Yes. Oh, that dreadful so-called nurse . . .'

'As well as the Colonel,' Holmes

added. 'It's — ' he broke off as the front door bell rang downstairs. 'That should be Lestrade.' He crossed to the door, opened it, and called down to Mrs. Hudson. 'That'll be Detective Inspector Lestrade, Mrs. Hudson.'

'Don't sound like him, Mr. Holmes,' her voice came back. 'He allus rings three times when he's expected . . . short, sharp ones.'

'That's so.' Holmes thought for a moment, then called down: 'Anyhow, answer the door and tell me who it is.'

'Yes, Mr. Holmes.' Mrs. Hudson opened the front door, then frowned as she saw who the visitor was. 'Oh, it's *you* again.'

'Good evening, Mrs. Hudson. Mr. Charles Augustus Milverton, at your service.'

Mrs. Hudson was unimpressed by the man's unctuous tone. 'Oh, yes?'

'Mr. Holmes is not expecting me, but — '

Watson had joined Holmes at the top of the stairs, where the voices downstairs reached clearly. He exchanged a look with

Holmes. 'It's Milverton! What can *he* want?'

Holmes called down: 'He can come up, Mrs. Hudson.' Then to Watson he added: 'Wait in the bedroom if you would. He probably thinks I'm alone, anyway.'

'Good idea,' Watson assented, and vanished into the bedroom.

'You can go on up,' Mrs. Hudson said shortly.

'Thank you, dear madam,' Milverton murmured, and started to climb the stairs to Holmes' room on the landing.

Milverton entered through the open doorway, and found Holmes standing by his writing desk. On it lay the gun-stick, it's butt end pointing towards the door.

'Mr. Holmes, good evening. It's most kind of you to permit me to call.'

'What d'you want?' Holmes said briefly.

Milverton indicated the gun-stick. 'My visit is to do with that thing's owner, as it happens.'

'If you mean Colonel Moran, he no longer owns it.'

'Nevertheless, he is anxious to have possession of it once more.'

'Has he deputed you to make an offer?' Holmes asked sharply.

Milverton shook his head. 'Let me explain. This afternoon, the Colonel received a visit from a criminal named Benskin, who claimed you'd hired him to do a deal on the basis that you'd exchange the gun-stick for Philip Green's release. Am I right?'

'I hear what you say,' Holmes replied guardedly.

'Then hear this!' Milverton's smooth voice took on a tone of sharp urgency. 'Despite any deal you may or may not have made with him, Colonel Moran intends to double-cross you . . . and wipe you off the face of the earth!'

'And when does he plan this interesting event?'

'Tonight!'

'How?' Holmes asked calmly.

'I don't know,' Milverton admitted. 'But my guess is Shlessinger and that sister of his will be involved.'

'And in return for your warning, how

do you expect me to reciprocate?' Holmes asked pointedly.

'Leave me out of it!' Milverton snapped. 'My attempt to blackmail Lady Frances; my association with the Shlessingers and Moran; forget it all.'

Holmes smiled grimly. 'You sound as if you have become somewhat scared of them.'

Milverton shrugged. 'I . . . I . . . well, perhaps I am becoming a little squeamish,' he admitted. 'Anyhow, I intend to take a holiday as far away from the aforementioned as possible.'

'Very wise, Mr. Milverton.' Holmes nodded. 'Well . . . thank you for your warning. I will reciprocate by forgetting this meeting ever took place and retaining not the slightest knowledge of your whereabouts or even existence.'

'Thank you,' Milverton said, his voice relieved. He extended his hand, but Holmes ignored it.

'Goodbye, Milverton . . . and good luck.' As Milverton turned to go out, Holmes added softly, almost to himself. 'I think you're going to need it.'

Milverton stopped and stared at Holmes for a long moment, then turned quickly and went out, leaving the door open behind him.

Holmes stepped forward and called down to Mrs. Hudson: 'Mr. Milverton is leaving, Mrs. Hudson.'

Mrs. Hudson looked at Milverton's hurrying figure in surprise. Without waiting for her to open the door he brushed past her and jerked it open himself.

The door slammed behind him.

On hearing it, Watson came in from the bedroom. 'What an extraordinary person,' he commented. 'I almost began to like him!'

Holmes smiled faintly. 'Your faith in human nature has always appealed to me as somewhat touching.'

Watson coughed. 'Well, I am a doctor . . . and faith is as helpful to a doctor as his stethoscope.'

'Quite so,' Holmes murmured..

'But what did you make of his story?'

Holmes shrugged. 'It was a sincere attempt to warn me, no doubt — but, of course, I already knew Moran would make another attempt to eliminate me . . . as well as retrieve his stick.'

'You already knew?' Watson looked his surprise.

Holmes nodded calmly. 'That was precisely why I allowed him to penetrate my disguise as Benskin.'

'Allowed him to penetrate your disguise?' Watson was incredulous. 'You mean, after all the trouble you took?'

'Indeed, it was a triumph . . . he was completely duped.'

Watson furrowed his brow. 'You mean that all the time, you wanted him to know it was you?'

'Not all the time,' Holmes admitted. 'But just before my exit, I let the mask fall.'

'How did you do that?'

Holmes reached into a pocket and pulled forth the £50 from his pocket. 'By accepting this from him.'

Watson stared. 'He offered you money?'

Holmes nodded. 'After a little haggling, he agreed to pay me £150 . . . £50 on account . . . ' He waved the £50 note,

' . . . if I obtained his gun-stick.'

Watson frowned. 'I still don't follow.'

'Allow me to demonstrate.' With his right hand Holmes extended the £50 note. 'Take this, if you would.'

Watson accepted the note. 'Well, it's a unique sensation . . . to hold such a large amount in one's hand . . . '

'Only temporarily, Watson!' Holmes smiled. 'Now, would you, as if you were Moran, give it me.' Wonderingly, Watson handed back the £50. 'Now, as I take it, do you observe anything about my hand?'

Watson looked down at Holmes' hand under his nose.

'Anything special? About my fingers? As a medical man you are used to dealing with all sorts of individuals.'

'Of course,' Watson said. 'Labourers, gentlefolk of both sexes, bank managers, greengrocers . . . '

'And a labourer's hand, for example . . . his fingernails wouldn't be as scrupulously clean as a bank-manager's?'

'His fingernails? No, of course not, they would be grubby, ill-kept.'

'And a burglar's?' Holmes prompted.

'Well, they would be . . . ' Watson broke off, staring at Holmes' right hand.

'Would you say they'd look like mine?' Holmes asked, putting on the voice he had used when posing as Benskin. 'Not long out of the 'Scrubs, Guv'nor . . . where I was sewing mailbags all the bleedin' day.'

'No, your nails are well-manicured . . . ' Watson paused. 'You deliberately showed Moran your hand, so he would realize . . . ?'

'Precisely.'

'My God, of course,' Watson said. 'He'll be out for revenge!'

'And to exact that revenge and retrieve his precious stick, he must face me — once again.'

'Here?' Watson questioned.

Holmes nodded. 'Where we faced each other a few hours back . . . and *this* time . . . '

Through the window drifted the sound of the barrel organ music they had heard before, only more distant.

'That barrel organ again,' Watson exclaimed. 'Only it's not in Baker Street.

It's in the street behind us.'

Holmes tensed. 'Yes . . . '

'Pity he doesn't know another tune.'

Holmes smiled, 'It is rather.'

Watson glanced at Holmes sharply. 'Why, it's another signal!'

The front door bell sounded again, this time with three short rings.

Mrs. Hudson called up from the hall. 'That'll be the Inspector this time, Mr. Holmes.'

Mrs. Hudson opened the door, admitting Lestrade. 'Good evening, Inspector.'

' 'Ello, Mrs. H.' Lestrade said briskly. As usual, he exuded purposeful self-confidence. ' 'Ere we are again.'

'You can go on up,' the housekeeper told him.

'Yes, I knows I'm expected, Mrs. H.' Lestrade strode forward and began ascending the stairs. 'It's Lestrade of the Yard,' he called up, and began whistling the tune played on the barrel organ.

Reaching Holmes' room he entered quickly. 'Good evening, Mr. Holmes — ah! And Dr. Watson, 'ere we are again, then.'

'Good evening.' Holmes and Watson responded in unison.

'Oh, by the way,' Lestrade went on briskly, 'I'm reliably hinformed, the Hon. Philip Green and his piece of crackling left, both wreathed in smiles and full of the joys of Spring.'

'Thanks to the efforts of Mr. Holmes on their behalf,' Watson remarked, as the sounds of the barrel organ outside died away.

Lestrade smiled. 'Ah, well, that's the best of being a private 'tec . . . no superiors to get under yer feet.'

'What's the news, Inspector?' Holmes asked sharply.

'My officers duly raided the Nursing Home,' Lestrade told him, 'only to find the Shlessingers . . . brother and sister . . . have vamoosed, cleared out, skipped the country. They left a note, saying in so many words, they would be absent for a long time.'

'Gone abroad?' Watson hazarded.

'Ah — that's what they want us to believe, Doc, but of course, Lestrade of the Yard has got his ear to the ground

. . . and I don't want no jokes about take care I don't get it trodden on!' He glared at Holmes as the detective smiled faintly and shrugged. 'And,' he resumed, 'my men are hot on the scent of the said absconding couple . . . ' he broke off as he noticed Holmes was now glancing at the ceiling. 'What's up?' he asked, puzzled.

'D'you hear something?' Holmes asked sharply.

Watson looked up. 'Footsteps,' he said.

Lestrade craned his neck upwards. 'I didn't hear anything . . . '

'Definitely footsteps,' Holmes told him. 'In the room above.'

They listened intently, then Watson broke the silence. 'They've stopped. I didn't know Mrs. Hudson let any other rooms, Holmes.'

'She has this evening.'

Lestrade frowned. 'Who to?'

'Listen!' The other two men joined Watson in gazing up again, listening intently.

'You're right,' Lestrade said. 'Someone's up there, no mistake. Let's get Mrs. H. up and find out who.' Crossing quickly to the doorway, he called down: 'Mrs. H. — would you come up?'

There was no response.

'I think if *I* asked her, it would be better,' Holmes said.

'Oh, sorry, Mr. Holmes . . . I didn't mean to . . . only, I'm anxious to know!'

Holmes called down: 'Mrs. Hudson!'

'Her Master's Voice!' Lestrade muttered,

'Yes, Mr. Holmes?' the housekeeper responded, after a short pause.

'Would you come up here for a moment, please?'

'Right away, Mr. Holmes.'

'The footsteps have stopped now,' Watson remarked, glancing up again.

'Mrs. H. should know something about those footsteps,' Lestrade remarked.

'They sounded like a woman's footsteps to me,' Watson said.

'Yes, Mr. Holmes?' Mrs. Hudson asked, entering the room.

'Someone's occupying the room above,' Holmes told her briefly. 'I didn't know you let other rooms?'

Mrs. Hudson appeared shocked. 'What?

Let other rooms? Oh, my goodness . . . oh, dear me.' She was clearly upset.

Watson crossed to her quickly. 'It's all right, Mrs. Hudson.'

'Oh, my goodness! I don't let other rooms . . . I mean . . . the gentleman you heard must be one of Ma Griffen's at 223.'

'They sounded like a woman's footsteps,' Lestrade said.

'A lady's?' Mrs. Hudson shook her head emphatically, clearly flustered. 'Oh, no, she only lets to gents. You see, she . . . Ma Griffen . . . oh, dear me . . . '

'Don't feel upset,' Holmes advised her gently. 'Just take it calmly.'

Watson offered Mrs. Hudson a chair, but she shook her head and remained standing.

'She's gone and let a room . . . at 223 . . . to a young chap and his brother for the evening.'

'What were their names?' Lestrade asked sharply.

'I don't know . . . she never said. They only want the room for this evening, you see . . . they told her they were catching the midnight to Edinburgh.'

'Could be the Shlessingers,' Lestrade commented.

Holmes raised an eyebrow. 'You think so?'

'Why not?' Lestrade said. 'The sister could have dressed as a man.'

Holmes turned to Mrs. Hudson. 'You didn't see them yourself, I suppose?'

'No . . . she told me earlier. What are they doing in my house?' Mrs. Hudson frowned. 'Oh, won't I have something to say to Ma Griffen, I can tell you!'

'How did they get in upstairs?' Lestrade said impatiently. 'That's the point!'

Mrs. Hudson considered for a moment, then said: 'Well, you see, there's a way across the roof from 223, and there's always been a faulty catch to that window what's never got properly mended . . . but I'll see to it, I promise, Mr. Holmes . . . oh, my goodness . . . to think of strangers upstairs — '

Holmes clapped a hand on her shoulder. 'Don't worry about it. Just carry on as if nothing has happened.'

'Yes,' Watson encouraged. 'Make yourself a nice cup of tea.'

Lestrade puffed himself a little. 'That's right, Mrs. H. Just leave everything to Lestrade of the Yard.'

Mrs. Hudson looked at him. 'Well! I do feel a bit of an 'eadache, coming on . . . '

Watson urged her gently towards the door. 'I can give you some aspirin.'

'No, no, Dr. Watson . . . thanks ever so. Just a cup of tea, and I'll be all right.' As she descended the stairs, she continued muttering to herself: 'Oh, dear . . . oh, fancy them getting into my house like that . . . '

Lestrade looked confidently at Holmes. 'Well, for my money, Ma Griffen's 'young man' is the Shlessinger female, while big brother waits for her at 223. Her dirty deed accomplished, they heads for destination unknown.'

Holmes shrugged. 'If you think so.'

Watson looked questioningly at Holmes, who shook his head.

Lestrade turned to the door. 'So, I just nips along and picks up Shlessinger, and see him off in my Sergeant's loving care

— and back pronto to help you deal with Miss Male Impersonator.' He jerked his thumb at the ceiling.

Just then the telephone rang.

Lestrade stopped and turned to Holmes. 'It may be my Sergeant . . . '

At Holmes' nod, Lestrade answered the telephone. 'Lestrade of the Yard here,' he said, then listened to the caller for a moment. 'What time was this?' he asked sharply. 'Where did the incident take place?' Pause. 'Well, it's as good a spot as any. Thanks, Sergeant. I'll be along in a minute.' Lestrade turned to Holmes, still holding the phone. 'We'll have no more trouble with Milverton.'

'Why, what's happened?' Watson asked.

'Been discovered in Melcombe Street, flat on his face, expiring his last.'

Watson gave a start. 'Murdered, d'you mean?'

'Considering he'd been shot in the back, it's not being treated as a case of suicide,' Lestrade said dryly. 'Incidentally, a young man was seen running away from the place at the relevant time.'

'A young man?' Watson frowned.

Lestrade raised the telephone. 'You still there, Sergeant . . . ? Pick up big brother, now. Yes, now . . . charge him with being an accessory to Milverton's come-uppance. Got it?' He hung up, then, as a sudden thought struck him, he gave a quick look at Holmes and continued talking as if he was still on the telephone. 'Wait a second, Sergeant . . . a cunning thought's occurred.' He darted another look at Holmes and glanced again at the ceiling. Raising his voice, he added: 'I'll be round pronto myself to see big brother on his way, and put out a search for the 'young man seen running away from the murder at the relevant time.' Got it, Sergeant? Good.' Still speaking loudly he continued: 'Well, Mr. Holmes, I'll nip round to 223 to see big brother on his way, and pick up his sister. So you can take it easy and all rest safe in your beds tonight.'

Holmes and Watson played up to Lestrade's stratagem, also speaking clearly.

'Good work, Inspector; we're most grateful to you.'

'Hear, hear!' Watson added heartily.

'Been a pleasure, I'm sure.' Lestrade exited noisily, calling over his shoulder at the door. 'Any time you got a problem, just send for Lestrade of the Yard.' He called out to Mrs. Hudson: 'Bye, bye Mrs. H. Hope your headache's better.'

'Oh, it is, Inspector, ever so much.'

'Sleep safe and sound, Mrs. H.'

Upstairs, Watson heard the front door open and shut. He looked at Holmes, speaking normally, 'The only thing that worries me now is Colonel Moran.'

'What about him?'

'Well, what's he up to? I can't believe he's given up trying to get his damned stick back.'

Holmes made no reply. Switching off the main light, he plunged the room into semi-darkness, and urged Watson into the bedroom, leaving the door half open. Then taking a small revolver out of his pocket, he half opened the main door to the landing, and positioned himself behind it.

Outside in Baker Street, a hooting taxi rattled past. Very slowly, the door began to open further. It stopped for a moment, then opened a bit more before stopping. As it opened wider Colonel Sebastian Moran moved silently as a shadow into the room.

Holmes flattened himself against the wall, gun in hand, his eyes fixed on Moran, who glided into the room.

At the same moment Lestrade appeared silently in the doorway behind the intruder, his attention fixed on Moran, who was now moving on tiptoe to the writing desk.

As Moran made a grab for the gun-stick, Holmes stepped quickly behind him, and rammed his gun in the man's back.

At the same moment Lestrade closed with Moran. The tussle caused the gun-stick to go off with a loud report, a bullet slamming into the wall just above the bedroom door.

Lestrade, benefitting from the element of surprise and Holmes' move with the revolver, succeeded in throwing Moran's gun to the floor, and dragging his hands behind him. There followed the clink of handcuffs being applied.

Watson appeared from the bedroom. Somewhat shakily, he looked towards the grimly smiling Yard man.

'I am Inspector Lestrade of Scotland Yard and I arrest you Colonel Sebastian Moran, on a charge of conspiracy to cause the death of Charles Augustus Milverton . . . '

'You all right, Watson?' Holmes questioned.

Watson managed a nod. 'So it wasn't Shlessinger or his sister,' he said.

'Never fear, Doctor,' Lestrade spoke confidently. 'I'll pick them up in no time.

'I had nothing to do with it,' Moran snarled. 'That murderous bitch took it into her head — '

' . . . And an attempt on the life of Dr. John H. Watson,' Lestrade finished implacably.

Watson glared at Moran as he moved in front of him, bent down and picked up the gun-stick. He handed it to Holmes as he moved across to face Moran.

Suddenly Holmes broke the gun-stick

savagely over his knee and threw the ends at Moran's feet.

Moran recoiled as if he'd been struck. 'I'll see you in Hell for that, Holmes. I'll see you in Hell!'

Lestrade jerked the handcuffed Moran round to face the door. 'Take it easy, Colonel — take it easy. You won't be seeing anyone in Hell for a long time, though they'll give you a taste of it in Dartmoor.'

As he was forced through the door, his cuffed hands behind his back, Moran turned and shouted at Holmes: 'You haven't seen the last of me, damn you, Holmes! We'll meet again . . . and next time . . . '

Watson stooped to pick up the broken gun-stick, and put the pieces into the wastepaper basket. '*What* a day it's been,' he mused. 'A beautiful woman being blackmailed . . . Her fiancé kidnapped . . . Milverton shot by that dreadful so-called nurse . . . and Moran creeping about, and damn near murdering me!'

As he was speaking Holmes crossed to the writing desk, and took out the hypodermic and phial from the drawer. He hesitated for a long moment, then replaced them and closed the drawer with a snap.

As Watson watched him intently, he picked up his violin, and started playing the same tune as that had been played on the barrel organ . . .

THE CASE OF THE
BURIED HATCHET

I opened the door with MARTIN BRETT on the frosted-glass panel and went in. He was standing by the window looking down at the street and as I crossed over I caught a glimpse below of the tall, plump figure that was Farringdon Tisdall get into a sleek limousine and drive off. The great financier had just left after half-an-hour's interview with Mr. Brett and the aroma of cigar hung expensively all over the office. He had also left a retaining-fee of mouth-watering magnitude, his personal cheque for which I placed on the desk.

'What it must be like to be filthy rich,' I said. I was thinking of how the money could set me up cosily in the way of frothy frillies and other girlish fancies.

'They tell me you can still sleep badly for all the cash in Farringdon Tindall's coffers,' Mr. Brett said over his shoulder.

I said: 'If you had that amount to spend

who'd worry about wasting time in bed.'

Still without turning his gaze from the direction the car had gone, Mr. Brett said, 'Perhaps you'll be intrigued to know you won't be climbing into your cot early tonight, anyway.'

Which brought from me a look of interest, plus surprise, plus slight apprehension. What job were we going on this time after office-hours? I said: 'Mr. Brett? Someone we know throwing a party?'

He came away from the window, moved slowly to his desk, tapped the ash off his cigarette. 'Farringdon Tisdall is,' he said. 'We're invited.'

'How awfully jolly of him,' I said as casually as I could. Though, of course, I was rather thrilled. I'd got a cunning little white number I hadn't worn since I bought it and this promised to be the sort of occasion where it should be put to the test. There'd be a really smart crowd there I knew. I'd heard of the kind of parties Farringdon Tisdall put on. Everything regardless. But inside that new gown and a hair-do — if my hairdresser could fit it in — I felt I could cope. I asked:

'What are we there for, to keep an eye on the silver?'

He handed me a small piece of paper. It had been torn from an ordinary writing pad and on it were gummed-in letters cut from a newspaper:

'DEAR SIR — SOMEOME WILL BE AFTER THE CRIMSON LAKE TONIGHT. THIS IS A WARNING FROM

A WELL-WISHER'

Mr. Brett explained; 'The Crimson Lake is a ruby, quite an expensive piece.' He nodded towards the bit of paper. 'He received that this morning.'

'Has he got anyone in mind?'

'Nobody in particular. But after he brushed off my suggestion mightn't it merely be a hoax, he pointed out there'll be two or three hundred guests stamping around tonight. Among them possibly one who simply can't wait to get his hands on the ruby.'

'I should have thought if he'd locked the thing away somewhere good and safe, he'd have nothing to worry about.'

He eyed the tip of his cigarette and said slowly: 'That did occur to me, too.'

There was a faintly derisive note in his voice, which made me glance at him sharply. But he only grinned at me enigmatically and bunged into the chair and put his feet up on the deck. I studied the warning message again in case I'd missed anything significant about it. I noticed the letters were neatly cut out and showed up with a pinkish edge to them against the white paper on which they'd been gummed. Nothing startling in all that though, and I looked inquiringly at Mr. Brett. His long face was as full of expression as a poker-playing mandarin — if mandarins play poker, which is something I've never asked about.

'I'm a girl of simple ideas,' I shrugged. 'So whatever it is goes on, goes on way over my head.'

'I didn't say anything.'

'It's what you're thinking.'

'Something tells me you evidently

suspect more in this than meets the eye.' He indicated Farringdon Tisdall's cheque. 'Personally, the only thing of any importance meets *my* eye is that. Which offers me the greatest inducement, so far, for taking on the job.' He paused. 'And yet somehow, Beautiful,' he went on — and I gave him the chill stare I always handed him when he used that familiar tone with me — 'I'm getting the idea there might be another interesting attraction to the case after all. Apart from this.' And he picked up the cheque and carefully put it in his wallet.

I didn't get his drift at all. But something had caused him to reach the conclusion he was going to have to work harder on the job this evening than merely prop up Farringdon Tisdall's buffet-bar. I had the smart idea the cheque had something to do with it. I'd never known him act like that over one before, tucking it away as if it were a vital clue or something. Always cheques were just put aside until I paid them into his account in the routine way. But this one was obviously more important than that.

How or why exactly I couldn't guess, so I waited for him to tell me more.

His eyes were narrowed as he said: 'I'll need all the dope on Tisdall pronto. Bill Foster will fix you up. You'll have to see him personally, so better organize it soon's you've had your lunch.'

'Yes, Mr. Brett.' I glanced at my wristwatch. 'If that'll be all for now, I'll start moving. It's about time to put on the nose-bag.'

He nodded. 'Dig up everything you can from the Tisdall files, and flutter your long eyelashes at Bill. When it comes to knowing the inside stuff on people, his big ear's closer to the ground than anyone in Fleet Street. Especially if it's dirty ground.'

I resented his suggestion I switched on the old eye-work business with men as being uncalled for and unnecessary. After all I can't help it if my eyelashes *are* long. But Mr. Brett always likes to get in a dig at my face or figure. Just because I don't happen to look like the back of a cab, and my curves happen in the right places. As I've probably mentioned before I have the

140

notion he sounds off that way on account of some secret sorrow, some woman in his past. Which is a pity, plenty fall for him who could help him forget that yesterday's memory if he'd give them the chance. But all they ever get from him is the sort of encouragement you'd give a cobra without its fangs drawn.

However, I just pretended not to notice he'd said anything I didn't like and said: 'I gather you think Mr. Tisdall may have a skeleton in his cupboard?'

'Now you come to mention it,' he said, 'I fancy I did catch the echo of something rattling back of his mind during our little chat. Or it may only have been the mice.'

And with a sardonic grin Mr. Brett stubbed out his cigarette and left it at that. I manhandled a sandwich and two cups of coffee at a cafeteria and grabbed a taxi for Fleet Street. As I paid it off outside the *Daily Courier* office I was just in time to catch Bill Foster coming through the swing doors. He was looking bigger and untidier than ever and whooped like a Red Indian when he saw me. He was going for a drink and a bite but when I told him what I was after he took my arm in his dear old breezy way and we went up in the lift to the newsroom. It was pretty quiet as newsrooms went and I parked myself on my desk and smiled graciously at a passing copy-boy who ogled my legs, while Bill got me the file on Farringdon Tisdall.

It was a fat file all right. Tisdall had stamped his dynamic personality on the world of finance in no uncertain way. With the cuttings on his meteoric business career went all the trimmings of his social climb. His yacht, his racing-stable, his country houses, villa on the Mediterranean, all the rest. Plenty about the Crimson Lake Ruby too. While I was working my way through it, scribbling notes of any stuff that looked particularly interesting for Mr. Brett, Bill ambled off and returned with another file, which he slapped down beside the other.

He watched my face as I stared at it, a bit puzzled. The name on the file was LYDIA DELMAR. Which didn't mean anything to me at all. Except it made me think of a name for some ice cream or something.

'Getting your names a bit mixed, Bill, aren't you?' I said.

He shook his head, his smile broader.

'You want the inside stuff as well, you said.'

I tapped the Delmar file. 'But where does she — ?'

'He was nuts about her,' Bill said.

Lydia Delmar's press-clippings were mostly photographs. Photos of an extremely delectable-looking blonde. The earlier captions underneath told you she was the well-known mannequin, and I began to remember I'd seen her in the smart fashion magazines. Then came some later photos of her smiling dreamily at a nice-looking dark young man with a sprinkle of confetti around his ears. The captions included his name, Raymond Ward. Bill Foster jabbed at him with his pipe-stem.

'He *used* to be Tisdall's private secretary.'

'Like that, was it?' I said.

'Like that,' Bill said. 'Chucked the big

143

man she did for the other one.'

'What's happened to them now?'

'Lydia's in New York working for some advertising firm, I believe. The boy's still around London, trying to scrape enough money to go out and join her.'

'Not much of a marriage, that.'

'Oh, I expect, they write each other. Often think marriages would work out better if the husband lived in one country and the wife in another.'

'You have the dearest ideas,' I told him.

He grinned back at me. Then he said reflectively, 'It knocked Tisdall all of a doodah. Some say he's never forgiven either of 'em. Hardly credit it, eh? Fact. All that dough and power couldn't buy him that little doll.' He jabbed Lydia Delmar's photo with his pipe. 'Course Tisdall kicked out young Ward on the spot. Real vicious he was. S'pose it hit his pride and all that.'

'Quite the dramatic stuff,' I said, taking a cigarette from my case. Bill held a match to it then applied it to his pipe. He puffed away thoughtfully for a moment, until the match he'd forgotten to blow out burned his fingers. Idly he turned some of the cuttings from the big file and picked out a photo of Tisdall.

'Talking of dramatics,' he said slowly, 'I always have the feeling one of these days I'll see that dial over a caption of quite a different kind.'

I looked at him curiously. 'How different?'

'I dunno,' he muttered. 'Something — *unpleasant.*'

I studied the face again with fresh interest. It wasn't a nice face, I thought and remembered that was the reaction I had when he'd come into the office that morning. It was puffy and the eyes were small and lidless. But staring at it now it didn't give me any reason to guess just how soon Bill Foster's prophetic words would be coming home like birds of ill-omen to roost.

When I got back Mr. Brett was in, looking very much the same as when I'd left him, with his feet still up on the desk. Just as if he'd never been out of the office. Automatically I expected to see the whisky-bottle at his elbow — he often stayed behind and took his lunch from that. But it was nowhere around. Instead there were several newspapers draped over everything, which weren't there before, so I knew he had in fact been out. I looked in again presently with the Farringdon Tisdall dope and he was staring at the anonymous message through a magnifying glass. Apparently he was comparing it with something in one of the newspapers. Then I noticed ail the papers were financial sheets. *The Financial Market, Daily Finance* and so on.

After a while it seemed to sink in I was in the same room with him and he turned and gave me a grin. 'How's it feel to watch the Great Sleuth at work?' He said, with that sarcastic jeer which was his own particular brand. 'Give you a thrill?'

'From where I'm standing, you look more like someone playing the Stock Market, in a crazy sort of way,' I said. 'Here's the stuff on Farringdon Tisdall.'

And I went back to my office to get on with the job of dealing with the mailing, the filing — the routine stuff which Mr.

Brett apparently fondly imagines is done by a troupe of tender-hearted pixies after I've locked up for the day.

After a while the speaking-machine on my desk crackled and his voice came at me like water sizzling over hot coals. 'Leave your lipstick and compact for now, Gorgeous, you're wanted.'

'Yes, Mr. Brett,' I said back into the box even more icily if possible than ever, and pulling a face at the darned thing. It *would* happen his jibe in the dark would catch me coincidentally just at the moment I'd paused to fix my make-up. I made an irritable grab for my notebook and went on in. He was by the window moodily contemplating the street. On a chair beside him was one of the newspapers, the warning letter and the magnifying glass. He turned to me and passed the newspaper, which was of a pink shade.

'Take a look at that.'

I saw at once part of a column he'd marked off with pencil. I puzzled at it, doing my best to appear as if it was making sense. Seemingly it was an extract from some company report, jam full of technical terms and references whose meaning was clear to me as mud. If it had been written in Aztec it couldn't have told me more.

'Very interesting,' I said.

'If you find that improving to the mind,' he grinned, 'this should kill you.' And handed me the letter. 'Take a peek at it, through this,' giving me the glass.

And then bingo I got what he was getting at.

The letters forming the warning message had obviously been cut out from an issue of the newspaper I'd just been looking at. Comparison proved that the type was identical with that of the pencilled column. Under the magnifying glass the pink edge I'd only half-noticed earlier on round each letter so neatly gummed to the writing paper was the exact shade of the newsheet.

Mr. Brett saw by my face that the penny had dropped. 'Came a great light,' he murmured sardonically.

'And what does it add up to?' I said.

He lit a cigarette and idly watched a

puff of smoke curl ceiling-wards, before he said slowly:

'It adds up to the possibility that the sender of the note warning Farringdon Tisdall his pet ruby was in danger of being pinched was himself a reader of the financial press. From which hypothesis — ' Mr. Brett cleared his larynx and his manner became almost expansive, sure sign he was beginning to enjoy listening to the sound of his own voice, ' — could evolve a logical sequence of questions. For example, what persons most interested in the ruby are also interested followers of newspapers devoted solely to finance? Having answered that one you could, by a narrowing-down process, proceed inevitably to put your finger on the party who sent the letter.'

'And when will you be taking *that* rabbit out of the hat?' I said. He regarded me with that derisive grin of his through another cloud of cigarette smoke.

'I'll do my utmost, Dream Girl,' he said, 'to show you the trick tonight.'

Farringdon Tisdall's house in Highgate

was a whacking great white mansion place standing in its own grounds screened from the road by trees, with a wide drive curving up to it. Mr. Brett didn't habitually claim the power of sixth sense, but on this occasion he seemed to have the idea nothing sensational would happen at the party before we appeared, so on our arrival the drive was already packed with opulent-looking cars, and I caught the sound of a dance-orchestra giving out as we went up the steps.

Coming back to the hall to find Mr. Brett after dumping my cape, I caught sight of a face that made me stop in my tracks. I'm pretty good at recognizing people and it was him all right. I must have been staring pretty hard. Anyhow he turned his head and stared back, finally giving me a tentative half-smile. I didn't reciprocate however, not with the idea of snubbing him, but because I was too preoccupied. I hurried on my way and found Mr. Brett standing somewhat aloof from the crowd milling round.

'Guess who I've just seen?' I said a trifle breathlessly.

'I'll buy it. Who?'

'Raymond Ward, the ex-secretary who pinched his girlfriend. Remember?' Well, not unnaturally I expected him to show some sign of surprise or even a mild interest, but all he did was to go a little bleak round the mouth and gaze past my left ear with a faraway expression.

'Wonder which way the bar is?' he said.

But before he could make a move a character with receding hair had come up and eyed him expectantly.

'Mr. Martin Brett?'

Mr. Brett nodded.

'My name is Selby. Mr. Tisdall's secretary.'

'Good,' Mr. Brett said, without any enthusiasm whatsoever.

Farringdon Tisdall had certainly taken no chances over the man he'd hired to take the place of young Ward.

Selby was a weedy-looking individual with thick-lensed spectacles and about as much appeal as a jellyfish.

I calculated there was practically no risk at all of him running off with anybody's girlfriend, except maybe another

151

jellyfish. And she'd have to be frantically hard up. He coughed apologetically, looked as if he was washing his hands without any soap, and said:

'Mr. Tisdall asked me to look out for you soon as you arrived. He would like to see you in the library.'

Mr. Brett said abruptly: 'Has he got any drink there?'

The secretary looked slightly startled, but recovered himself to smile thinly. 'I'm sure Mr. Tisdall will be able to offer you some refreshment.'

Mr. Brett threw him a nod and we trailed off to the library. Farringdon Tisdall greeted us with quite a show of affability and, with a cigar which looked about three feet long stuck in his face, began pouring out the drinks. As he handed them to us, he said:

'I thought we might have a chat and if there's anything you'd like to know that would be useful . . . ' He left the rest of the sentence suspended on the cigar smoke and looked helpful.

Mr. Brett let his gaze take in the surroundings over the rim of his glass.

And Farringdon Tisdall's library was something that you really had to take in. Luxury literally leered at you from every side. Rich oak panelling from floor to ceiling, curtains and tapestries that glowed with gorgeous colour and a carpet so thick you felt you were walking in velvet up to your ankles.

After a moment Mr. Brett said: 'Where's the ruby tucked away?'

The other crossed obediently to the wide fireplace and then pressed somewhere underneath the massive ornately carved mantelpiece. At his touch a section of the woodwork about nine inches square sprang open to reveal a small wall safe. 'Neat isn't it?' Mr. Tisdall said over his shoulder. He went on: 'Needless to say we in this room are the only people who know of its existence.'

Mr. Brett glanced casually at Selby who'd remained unobtrusively in the background, making no contribution to the conversation and doing precious little to improve the scenery either. Now, however, he ventured to put his oar in with:

'*And* my predecessor.'

'Ah yes,' Farringdon Tisdall murmured as if reminded of the fact. His face took on an abstract expression, then he seemed to dismiss whatever it was he'd been thinking and bent slightly in an attitude of concentration before the safe.

There was a sharp metallic click and the safe-door swung back. Mr. Tisdall rummaged inside and after a moment held the Crimson Lake under the light for our inspection. It was beautiful, glowing up at us like something alive. I cooed the usual assortment of appropriately admiring remarks while Mr. Brett, his thoughts for all I knew wandering round the wilds of Tibet or somewhere, gazed at it as if it was a bit of coloured glass.

Then Farringdon Tisdall looked up and said conversationally: 'By the way, Mr. Selby's — er — predecessor already referred to happens to be one of my guests tonight.' He smiled slowly but it seemed to me it didn't quite match up with his lidless eyes. 'Yes,' he went on smoothly, 'the circumstances of his leaving were somewhat painful to me at the time, but I hope all that's forgotten now. And forgiven. His presence here is in fact an attempt on my part to persuade him to let bygones be bygones. Ward his name is, Raymond Ward. Charming and very able young man.' He considered a moment while Mr. Brett and I didn't bat an eyelash, though what we were hearing hardly added up to the inside-story tipped off to me by Bill Foster. Mr. Tisdall was continuing: 'I feel I was perhaps too harsh on him. After all, one shouldn't forget the time when oneself was young — ' He broke off and turned to Selby: 'Mr. Ward has arrived?'

'Er — yes,' the other nodded.

'Perhaps you'd find him presently and say I'd be glad for him to join me over a drink?'

'Very well.' He hesitated for a moment and then muttered: 'If you'll excuse me, there are one or two other matters I have to attend to.'

After he'd gone, Mr. Brett said: 'Presumably your secretary has some idea why we're here?'

'He knows who you are, yes. No one

else does, of course.'

'And the letter?'

'I told him about that — I saw no reason why I shouldn't. Why?'

'No reason at all,' Mr. Brett agreed amiably.

He began to wander apparently aimlessly round the room drawing abstractedly at his cigarette. I had worn out all the superlatives I could think up over the ruby, and there was a little silence. Mr. Tisdall glanced at Mr. Brett over his cigar, shot a glance of inquiry at me, which I answered with a beaming smile, leaving him to make what he liked of it, and he crossed over to the safe with the ruby. As he bent to close it up he said over his shoulder: 'Of course, as an added precaution I switch the combination every two or three days. Only Selby and I know what it is.'

The remark was intended for Mr. Brett, who, however, appeared to have lost what little interest he'd ever had in the jewel and was, I saw from the corner of my eye, glancing idly through some magazines and newspapers on a table. I covered up his unresponsiveness by blathering something about what a smart idea it was for Mr. Tisdall to take the extra precaution.

And then Mr. Brett spoke from the other side of the room, very quietly. 'No risk of either of you jotting down the combination and leaving it about for anyone else to see?' he asked, which just shows what a mistake it is to kid yourself he ever lets a darn thing get past him, no matter how much you think his mind's on something else at the time.

The other replied that the combination was simple enough to remember, no need to write it down, you just kept it in your head. A few minutes later we left Farringdon Tisdall in the library and Mr. Brett complaining he was still thirsty, was pushing off in the direction of what he hoped was a bar. On our way we saw Selby talking to Raymond Ward and they passed us, presumably going to the library. The secretary peered at us shortsightedly with a nod of acknowledgement, while the other looked at me as if he'd like to give me that tentative half-smile again.

Mr. Brett leant against the bar for a surprisingly short time and I trailed after him back to the hall. He lit a cigarette for me, then his own, and I listened to the dance-music watching the celebrities, and those who thought they were, passing to and fro, while he fixed his eyes in a basilisk stare on the passage leading to the library. Presently he relaxed somewhat and Raymond Ward appeared.

Mr. Brett went purposefully over to him.

'Mr. Ward?'

The other said: 'Yes,' saw me and definitely brightened. Mr. Brett cut out the fancy work, said straight away who he was.

'Think a quiet little chat is indicated,' he said, while Ward was recovering from his surprise, and led the way over to a secluded corner behind the wide staircase. There was a sudden air of urgency about him which made me give him a sideways glance.

'First,' he said briskly, 'hasn't it struck

you as slightly incongruous your being here tonight?'

Ward caught the unmistakable implication behind the question. 'You mean him inviting me — of all people?' And went on: 'Well he phoned and said he was prepared to forget what happened, let bygones be bygones and all that, if I felt the same way about it. *He* wanted to bury the hatchet, he said, and would I come to this party and we'd shake hands over a drink. So — well — I don't go in for bearing malice and here I am.'

'You didn't think this idea might be to bury the hatchet in you?' Mr. Brett said, and the other looked at him sharply.

'What d'you mean?'

'Never mind,' Mr. Brett waved the idea aside. 'So you've been having a drink and Farringdon Tisdall's been magnanimous all over the library. Quite like old times, eh?'

Ward grinned. 'Roughly that,' he said. 'He asked after Lydia — my wife you know.' He hesitated and said: 'He and Lydia were — '

'I know,' cut in Mr. Brett.

'Matter of fact, it *was* quite like old times.' And he laughed, as if something had amused him. 'He even asked me to show him an old handkerchief trick that used to peeve him because he could never do it.'

'What handkerchief trick?'

'Tie it so it looks like a rabbit. He always made a hash of it. Even when he tried it just now.'

I noticed the handkerchief protruding from his breast pocket looked a little crumpled.

Mr. Brett's face suddenly froze. Then:

'I'm interested in tricks,' he said softly. 'Show.'

Raymond Ward smiled and proceeded to oblige. As he pulled the handkerchief out something slipped from its folds and lay in the palm of his hand. He stared at it stupidly.

'Some trick,' murmured Mr. Brett as the Crimson Lake ruby gleamed up at us. He grabbed it. 'Wait here,' he snapped at the other, who was still glassy-eyed as if he'd been kicked smartly in the stomach by a recalcitrant mule, and was gone.

I managed to catch up with him as he reached the library and followed him in, to be brought up with a sickening shock. Farringdon Tisdall hadn't in my opinion made a particularly pretty picture before, but now slumped over his writing desk with his head bashed in he was a ghastly sight. Mr. Brett had already crossed to him.

'Is he dead?' I asked, my voice sounding as if it belonged to someone else.

He nodded grimly, glanced at a hefty-looking ornament — which could have done the job — sprawled on the desk amongst scattered papers and capsized inkstand from which green ink had spilled and was staining the gorgeous carpet. He jabbed a bell push and then I followed his look across to where the wall safe gaped wide-open. My brain was spinning round in crazy circles as I tried to make sense of what must have happened. It seemed fantastic to believe Raymond Ward could have done this terrible thing, yet — My bewilderment was momentarily interrupted as Selby hurried into the room. He stared unbelievingly at the figure at the desk then swayed and seemed as if he was about to collapse only Mr. Brett brought him up with a jerk.

'Get the police,' he said curtly.

'But — but a doctor?' the secretary gasped as he moved like a sleepwalker to the phone.

'Needn't worry about that for the moment. Police.'

Selby mumbled incoherently and lifted the receiver. Mr. Brett stared across at him through a puff of cigarette smoke and said slowly: 'I'll talk to 'em. *And you'd better make it good.*'

My heart seemed to stop in that dreadful silence as Selby blinked over the receiver and mouthed: 'What — what d'you mean?'

'Only you knew that combination beside Tisdall. Trouble was, when you opened the safe you were too late. He'd already planted it on young Ward.' He thrust his hand into his pocket and brought out the Crimson Lake. 'That's what you were after, wasn't it?'

Selby's face was drained putty-colour. 'I — I haven't been in here since Ward,' he rasped.

'That won't do either,' Mr. Brett smiled bleakly. 'Look at your shirt cuff.'

The other sucked in his breath and peered short-sightedly at his hand clutching the phone. *The cuff showing above it was stained with ink, bright green.*

★　★　★

'Of course,' said Mr. Brett in the taxi later, 'Selby planned the whole thing with the idea suspicion would fall on Ward. Mere fact Ward hadn't the ruby on him wouldn't necessarily clear him — police could argue he'd hidden it to collect later. But what Selby didn't know was Tisdall had invited ex-secretary for sole purpose of planting ruby on him, then accusing him of theft.'

'Motive: revenge?'

'Just that. Tisdall himself concocted anonymous warning as excuse to have me on the spot when his scheme went into operation. I confirmed my earlier hunch on that score when I took a peek at his papers in the library. Remember the financial sheet, type identical with gummed letters of note? Tisdall had an issue of that paper, with bits cut out of it.'

I murmured something appropriately appreciative of Mr. Brett's talents. Mr. Brett, who was beginning to wallow in the sounds from his own vocal chords, again went on: 'He planted the stone when Ward was doing the handkerchief trick. Selby, moment the boy goes, pops into library, socks Tisdall and then discovers he's done dirty deed for nothing. No ruby. So he beats it. The rest . . . ' And he allowed the rest to melt into cigarette smoke.

I remembered something. 'What about your cheque?' I asked. 'Now Farringdon Tisdall's no longer with us?'

Mr. Brett smiled at me derisively from the darkness of the taxi. 'Cashed it this morning. When I went out to get the papers. Just an idea I had something inconvenient might happen to my client.'

THE CASE OF THE
BORGIA RELIC

'Mr. Martin Brett's office,' I said automatically as I lifted the receiver,

'My name is Gale, Edwin Gale.' The voice over the wire had a pleasing resonance. 'I wonder when is the earliest I could see Mr. Brett? It's pretty urgent, I'm afraid,' he said, a note of anxiety edging his tone.

'He's awfully busy,' I said dubiously, cocking an eye towards the half-open door which had MARTIN BRETT on the frosted-glass panel and beyond which Mr. Brett was tilted back in a chair his feet on the desk idly blowing smoke-rings at the ceiling.

'Couldn't he possibly fit me in this afternoon?' the other urged. 'I — er — that is, I think I could make it worth his while.'

I made my voice sound as if I was wearing a slightly bored smile. 'That would hardly influence Mr. Brett if his

167

appointment diary is already full,' I purred.

He was suitably impressed — they always were when I gave 'em that line — and quickly tried to cover up his clumsy attempt at persuasion. 'Quite, quite,' he jerked out. 'What I mean is — well — I need his help quickly, or it'll be too late. And if there was some way in which he *could* manage to — that is — well, I really am in a hellish fix — '

I interrupted his floundering. 'Will you hold on a moment, please, Mr. Gale, I'll just see if there is a chance — '

'I'd be most grateful,' he said, brightening. 'Any time this afternoon — '

I left the receiver on my desk and went into Mr. Brett, closing the door after me. 'A Mr. Gale on the phone with something on his mind,' I told him.

He didn't take the slightest notice, just puffed another smoke-ring and watched it rise with somewhat morose concentration. He hadn't been in the best of moods all morning. Maybe it was because he was a little edgy on account of an arduous and extremely tricky case he'd been working

on and just cleared up after a painstak-
ingly involved investigation. This private
detective business isn't all fun and games
with a neat, dramatically clean-cut climax
by a long chalk. Too often it's a sordid,
wearing racket and dirty all the way
through. And even though the fee was a
fat one I knew Mr. Brett hadn't enjoyed
this last little job at all. Or again maybe it
wasn't that either. Maybe he'd just been
reminded, for some reason that I
wouldn't know about, of that secret
sorrow of his. I've mentioned it before,
my intuition that there's been some
woman in his past.

Anyway, I said patiently: 'He wants to
know if you'll see him this afternoon.
Sounds pretty het-up, if you ask me.'

He said without turning his head: 'I'd
be more interested to know what sort of a
sound his cheque will make.'

'I think he's the kind that talks money,'
I said. (As I believe I've also mentioned
before, Mr. Brett runs his business on
strictly business lines, none of the
amateur gumshoe who snoops round
outsmarting the police just for the hell of

it about him. And if that doesn't sound so glamorous as those clever-clever sleuths you read about in books, that's too bad.)

Mr. Brett gave me his saturnine smile. 'All right,' he said, 'if you say so,'

'Three this afternoon?'

He nodded.

'Yes, Mr. Brett,' I said and went out. I picked up the phone and cooed: 'So sorry to keep you waiting, Mr. Gale — '

'Oh, that's all right. Have you managed to fix anything?'

'I've had a word with Mr. Brett and he finds he could see you at three o'clock this afternoon,'

'Splendid, splendid. I really am most awfully grateful to him. Three o'clock? I'll be there on the dot. And again thank you very, very much.'

Mr. Gale arrived at five minutes to three and outwardly at any rate confirmed the impression he'd given me over the phone that he was the type who talked money. He was middle-aged plump and immaculately dressed in astrakhan-collared coat and black Homburg. Of course, I'm not mug enough to be fooled just by the way a prospective client is dolled up, astrakhan coat can hide an empty tummy and an even emptier bank-account. I know. But Edwin Gale looked to me as if besides his opulent exterior his pockets were very nicely lined, too.

He gave me a charming smile when I asked him to park himself, Mr. Brett would be free in a moment, and produced a gilt and cream box from his pocket which he handed to me. My heart fairly bounced with excitement as I opened it and goggled at the ornately carved bottle of perfume inside. It was quite the most wildly expensive stuff I'd ever seen at such close quarters. He was saying:

'Your voice seemed to tell me somehow yours was the personality that particular perfume would suit. And,' with a glance that was meant to be veiled but which I could read like a book, 'I'm not disappointed. I hope you aren't either?'

'It's very kind of you,' I said,

'Merely a slight repayment of your kindness to me this morning,' he murmured. 'I need Mr. Brett's aid quite desperately.' His face clouded for a moment. Then he smiled again and with a nod to towards the gift said: 'I hope you'll accept it — that is, unless your mother has absolutely forbidden you to take presents from strange men?'

I laughed in what I hoped was a delightful way. 'My mother never said anything about such a lovely present as this,' I said, removing the stopper and breathing in deeply. He was laughing, too, and then the speaking-machine on my desk clicked alive and Mr. Brett's sardonically familiar tones crackled at me.

'When you're through laughing at Mr. Gale's funny stories, Gorgeous, perhaps you'll show the gentleman in.'

'Yes, Mr. Brett,' I said with all the icy hauteur I could freeze into my voice. I turned to Mr. Gale who was looking at me with raised eyebrows and flashed him my most radiant smile. 'Mr. Brett will see you now.'

Mr. Brett told me to stay and take notes while he waved the other into a seat and indicated to him to get down to business pronto.

'I'm a collector and dealer in rare books. My business is an exclusive one and carried out by private transactions with other individual collectors, though on occasions, when I happen to acquire an appropriate rarity, I do deal with museums and famous libraries. However, as I say, it's mostly through private channels.'

Edwin Gale coughed, hesitated, crossed a perfectly creased trouser-leg over the other and came to the point. 'Recently a most wonderful rarity came into my possession: The Secret Memoirs of Caesar Borgia, written during his imprisonment in Spain, 1496-1506. A priceless relic as you may well imagine.'

'I can imagine somebody borrowing it and forgetting to return it, if that's what you mean,' Mr. Brett said,

The other nodded grimly. 'You have grasped the situation at once.'

'That's what I'm paid for,' Mr. Brett said briskly. 'Any idea who the absent-minded — er — booklover is in this case?'

Mr. Gale hesitated a moment before he said slowly: 'I am pretty certain though I can't be positive.'

'What's his name and why d'you suspect him?'

'His name's Spencer. Vere Spencer. A young man, rather likeable as a matter of fact. A woman friend of mine brought him to a little party I gave last week at my flat. In the course of a conversation we had together he told me he was interested in my line of business, suggested he sometimes acted as a sort of agent for collectors and if I ever had anything which he might be able to do something about would I let him know and all that sort of thing. I mentioned this volume of Borgia Memoirs. He seemed very keen, begged me to let him see the book. So I took him along to my study. He was vastly intrigued by the relic, said he'd get in touch with one or two people he knew quietly and he might be able to effect a deal to our mutual satisfaction. I didn't take him very seriously, but told him if an attractive offer came via him, well, I would, of course, consider it. Afterwards, when my guests had gone, the book was nowhere to be seen.'

'Did you lock it away after you'd shown it to Spencer?'

'I'm afraid I omitted to. I returned it to the drawer in my desk and forgot to turn the key.'

'That was careless of you, wasn't it, Mr. Gale. I presume it was possible for Spencer to slip into the study during the party and pinch the book?'

'That is what I suspected has happened,' he admitted.

'When did this occur?'

'A week ago.'

'Why so long calling me in?'

'Well, it was rather embarrassing. I couldn't be *certain* Spencer had taken the Memoirs. It might have been one of my other guests.'

'Or a servant?'

He shook his head. 'My manservant has been with me too long, he has my complete confidence. While the daily help is, of course, ruled out.'

'Who else of the guests might have been implicated?'

Again that slight hesitation. Then: 'I'm afraid there is no one. They were all personal friends of mine and I cannot believe any of them would have been capable of — of robbing me.'

Mr. Brett regarded him for a moment. Then he said through a cloud of cigarette-smoke: 'You mentioned that Spencer was brought along by a woman. Did she know much about him?'

'He was an acquaintance of hers, that's all. She'd understood he was something of a collector and thought I might like to meet him. I — I rang her up the following morning, as a matter of fact, and informed her what had happened. She lunched with me later and I told her frankly what I suspected. She was very upset, naturally, but was inclined to agree with me that Spencer could be the only one who might have stolen the book.'

'Which would seem to imply you haven't considered the possibility that she and Spencer were in this together.'

Mr. Gale looked startled for a moment. 'Good gracious, no,' he exclaimed. 'Nothing like that about it, I assure you. It was sheer misfortune that he'd made her acquaintance and she'd introduced him to me. That is,' he added hurriedly, 'assuming Spencer to be a thief.'

'Your story plus a process of elimination makes the assumption a pretty sound idea,' said Mr. Brett,

'I suppose you're right.'

'So you'd like me to recover your property. By the way,' with a nod in my direction, 'my secretary said you wanted to see me urgently. Why the sudden rush, after taking a week to think it over?'

'I have a purchaser for the Memoirs,' the other said simply. 'An American who's going back to New York first thing tomorrow. He leaves London by the boat-train tonight and would have taken the book with him.'

'As a matter of interest, or call me nosey, how much would you be soaking him for it?'

Mr. Gale froze slightly. Then he shrugged and said stiffly: 'Five thousand pounds,'

'No wonder you're steamed up,' Mr. Brett smiled thinly. 'If I can get the thing back for you by tonight you'll rake in quite a wad. Five thousand quid, just for an old book,' he murmured thoughtfully and added: 'Less my fee.'

Edwin Gale said: 'This is my suggestion, Mr. Brett. That you satisfy yourself Spencer has the Borgia relic in his possession and offer him five hundred pounds for its return, no questions asked. If you are successful I suggest two-fifty pounds for your trouble.'

Mr. Brett examined the tip of his cigarette. The other watched him silently. After a moment Mr. Brett looked up and said: 'I'll take the case, half of the fee to be paid down now, rest on delivery of the Memoirs in time to catch the boat-train tonight,'

Gale produced his cheque-book.

'Cash preferred,' Mr. Brett smiled at him. He added: 'I expect Spencer'll want his that way, too.'

The other stared at him his mouth compressed, then without a word took out his notecase. Mr. Brett gave me a nod. 'Take care of the gentleman's money,' he said.

'If you'll come this way, Mr. Gale,' I smiled at him graciously, 'I'll give you a receipt.' I felt quite indignant on his behalf. Mr. Brett had been quite unnecessarily brusque with him, I thought. But then Mr. Brett never went out of his way to be sweetly polite to his clients. The curious thing was that they seemed to be impressed by his snappiness. Which was probably precisely why he behaved that way. He was lounging back with his feet up on the desk again and calling after me: 'Mr. Gale will give you his address and phone number where I can get him any time. Also Spencer's address and number.'

'Yes, Mr. Brett,' I said.

After Edwin Gale had gone, leaving me with a nice, friendly smile, the speaking-machine on my desk crackled again and I went back to Mr. Brett. 'Well,' I said, 'you must admit I wasn't so far wrong when I told you he'd be the type who talked money.' I didn't mention anything about the perfume I'd had given me, he'd only have made some sarcastic remark. 'And,' I went on, 'it looks as if it's going to be one of the easiest two-fifty pounds you ever earned. Just persuade this man Spencer he's got an old book that doesn't belong to him, buy it back with someone else's cash, and the job's done.'

'Money for old rope, isn't it?' he said easily. But there was an enigmatic smile at the back of his eyes made me suddenly wonder if he was meaning what he said. He glanced at his wristwatch and murmured: 'I'll be paying a call on the character in question presently. You'd better tag along, that exotic personality of yours may help distract him, make it easier for me to winkle out the Memoirs.' And then he added: 'You might dab some of that perfume his nibs gave you behind the ears, they tell me it's wildly intriguing.'

I stared at him open-mouthed. How the devil did he know about my nice present? Was he psychic, or had his ear been at the keyhole when Mr. Gale was waiting in my office? But he was only grinning at me in that infuriating way he had and I realized I was merely looking foolish gaping at him. I closed my mouth so quickly I bit my tongue and went out slamming his door after me. To this day I don't know how he knew about that perfume.

Vere Spencer lived in a small mews flat off Oxford Street. On the corner of the mews Mr. Brett spotted a telephone box. I followed him over to it. I heard him dialling a number and wait for some time. No reply. He dialled again — presumably to make sure he'd got the right number — still no answer. He came out of the box and gave a nod of satisfaction.

'He's out,' he said. He glanced up and down. The mews was deserted, and we crossed to the flat, quickly ascending the short iron stairway. 'Keep your eyes and ears wide,' he snapped and turned his back to me. I watched, ready to warn him of the appearance of anyone who might be Spencer, and heard the metallic rattle of those odd-looking keys he sometimes carried as he got to work on the front door. In a few minutes there was a click of the lock and he pushed the door open.

He paused on the threshold and said over his shoulder: 'If he shows up while I'm taking a look round give me a quiet call and remember we've mistaken his flat for a friend's, found the door left unlocked — '

'The old routine,' I interrupted him.

'The old routine,' he said, and went in.

He seemed to be ages, with me every moment expecting someone to appear in the mews, forcing me to tip him off. But only a couple of stray cats slunk into view, plus a whistling errand-boy who drifted in for a quiet smoke and then drifted off again. When Mr. Brett reappeared and closed the door carefully behind him my watch told me he'd taken actually only twelve minutes on the job. In which time I knew he'd gone through the flat with a fine toothcomb, at the same time leaving not the faintest sign that anyone had been anywhere near the place. Light-fingered wasn't the word for it when Mr. Brett snooped around. I saw from his face he'd discovered all he needed to discover from his search of Vere Spencer's flat,

We turned into Oxford Street and grabbed a taxi. He leaned back and lit a cigarette. He said: 'I'm dropping you at the office. I'm going on to Scotland Yard.'

'Scotland Yard?' I stared at him blankly.

'But I thought Mr. Gale hired you because he wanted to keep the police out of this?'

He smiled at me bleakly through a puff of cigarette smoke, 'I think you've got something there,' he said. I didn't get it all. I said: 'Did you find the precious book?'

He nodded. 'I found it. 'Secret Memoirs of Caesar Borgia Set Down In His Hand, 1496–1506'. I only had time for a quick peek at it,' he went on, 'but it looked pretty interesting.'

'Isn't Borgia the chap who dodged around poisoning people on the slightest provocation?'

'He was practically the originator of the cocktail, I'm told,' Mr. Brett said absently. I glanced at him sharply. Either some natty little scheme was unwrapping itself behind that faraway look or he'd merely been reminded he could do with a drink, and was deciding on a dive to pop into on his way to Scotland Yard.

When he dropped me at the office he said: 'Be outside the mews in a couple of hours' time. That little heart-to-heart with Spencer is on the schedule just the same and I'll still want you around to lend your glamour to the conversation.' And he leered at me from the taxi.

'Yes, Mr. Brett,' I said with my nose in the air, and he pushed off.

I was there waiting for him on the corner of the mews when he got out of his taxi and loomed up out of the dusk.

'Spencer's at home now,' I was able to tell him. 'There's a light in the window and I caught a glimpse of a man in the flat, I took it to be him.'

He grinned at me over the glowing tip of his cigarette. 'So you do sometimes have an eye for business other than how your frock's showing off your figure,' he said. Which coming from him was quite a compliment.

The man I'd seen in the flat opened the door to us. He was wearing a dressing gown over his evening shirt and a long cigarette-holder stuck from the corner of a thin mouth. He stared at us and his expression didn't exactly exhibit wild delight at our presence.

'Who are you, and what d'you want?'

Mr. Brett told him who we were. 'A certain Mr. Gale is wondering if you've finished with the book you borrowed, because he'd like it back.' He added: 'If you were polite, you'd invite us in.'

The other hesitated, then glanced down at Mr. Brett's foot which was strategically placed to prevent the door being closed. He shrugged and stood aside. It was a comfortably furnished flat, and its owner obviously wasn't doing so badly out of the book-borrowing business. He was saying: 'I don't quite get what you mean about my having anything belonging to Mr. Gale, perhaps you can be a bit more explicit?'

Mr. Brett smiled agreeably. 'A week ago you pinched a volume from him entitled 'The Secret Memoirs of Caesar Borgia'. It's a valuable relic and I'm hired to get it back. It's as simple as that, really.'

Spencer smiled with excessive charm. 'It would be — if I knew what in hell you were talking about.'

Mr. Brett stifled a tiny yawn of boredom and said, his tone slightly weary: 'You'll find it in that bureau in the corner.

Second left-hand drawer. Save a lot of argument if you came across.'

Spencer nearly swallowed his cigarette-holder in his astonishment. Involuntarily he betrayed his knowledge of the whereabouts of the stolen property by backing in the direction of the bureau as if to ward off any movement towards it. He pulled himself up with a jerk as he realized the significance of his action and stared at us with a baffled expression.

Mr. Brett regarded him with a saturnine smile. He murmured:

'Maybe I should mention that in return for the Memoirs I'm to hand you five hundred quid cash, no questions asked.'

The other's aggressive attitude relaxed. He smiled — it made me think of a wolf about to walk into a flock of lambs — and drew calmly at his cigarette. He eyed the spiral of smoke curling from the holder and said: 'Mr. Gale is more than generous. You say you've brought the money with you?'

Mr. Brett gave me a nod, and I took a thick bundle of notes from my handbag. Mr. Brett took them from me and held them up for the other's inspection.

'Well, of course,' Spencer said slowly, his gaze riveted on the wad of money, 'that does seem to jar the memory, somewhat.'

'You must be kidding,' Mr. Brett jeered at him.

Spencer's grin stretched wider, then he turned to the bureau. He pulled open the drawer Mr. Brett had indicated and drew out what I saw was a book, extremely battered and ancient in appearance. 'I fancy this may be what Mr. Gale's thinking of,' he said casually over his shoulder. And then suddenly turned with a swift movement and crouched before us, a nasty-looking automatic in his other hand. 'Only he's not getting it back — yet,' he snarled. 'Not until he's a bit *more* generous. To the tune of another five hundred, shall we say?'

He moved towards us, jerking the gun at Mr. Brett. 'I'm taking the cash you've so kindly brought on account,' he said. 'Put it on the table and then get out.'

I didn't like the way the tables had been turned on us at all and threw Mr.

Brett a quick glance to see how he was taking it. To my surprise he pushed the money into his pocket and was lighting a cigarette as casually as you please. As a study in sheer nonchalance it made a pretty enough picture, but to my mind it seemed the wrong moment to pose for it — Spencer's ugly gun looked much too liable to go off — and if Mr. Brett wanted a cigarette surely he could wait till he *and* I were out of range. Now he was saying quietly:

'Nifty-looking device you have there, Spencer. Pity it happens to be unloaded.'

I gave a gasp and threw a look at Spencer, saw him press the trigger with a harmless clicking sound as the only result. Then I realized what must have happened and almost laughed out loud. Mr. Brett had taken the precaution of emptying the gun during his snoop-round earlier He was smiling bleakly himself as he watched Spencer still pulling foolishly at the trigger, then livid-faced throw it down in enraged disgust. Then Mr. Brett didn't look amused any more, he snapped his fingers and motioned the other to pass over the Borgia Memoirs. Spencer shrugged his acceptance of defeat and obeyed with a wry grin. Mr. Brett pocketed the precious book.

'I fear,' he said blankly, 'that in view of your somewhat uncooperative attitude my client's five hundred pound offer no longer stands.' And he handed the crisp bundle back to me. I felt Spencer's gaze follow me as I slipped it into my handbag again. I thought he started to say something, but he appeared to content himself with giving Mr. Brett a dirty look and let it go at that.

Not that Mr. Brett seemed to mind for he turned to him with a smile that was almost affable. 'Which I think,' he said, 'just about clinches the — er — transaction. I'm sure my client will be duly pleased with the safe return of his property,' patting his pocket.

A curious expression which I took to be a spasm of rage flickered across the other's face and was gone. Then he said in distinctly uncivil tones: 'Get the hell out of here, both of you.'

Well, there being no reason at all for us to stay, we didn't.

I followed Mr. Brett as he moved quickly out of the mews. He paused at the phone-box on the corner. 'What's my client's number?' I told him and waited outside while he telephoned.

He was a few moments talking to Edwin Gale, and when he hung up I heard him dial again. This time he asked for Inspector Conway's extension and while I was puzzling over why he could be dragging Scotland Yard into it, I heard him speaking briskly to the Inspector and caught the name 'Clifford Lang' and the Hotel Magnifique. He rang off and as he came out of the box I glimpsed the grin on his face. It was all very mysterious but I didn't ask him a thing until we were in the taxi and he'd told the driver to make it snappy to the Hotel Magnifique.

'And who — just in case I mightn't guess — would be expecting you, at the Magnifique?'

'My client, who is already on his way there, will, together with the prospective purchaser of this volume, be eagerly awaiting my arrival.'

'The American who's catching the boat-train?'

'Exactly. An individual of means named Clifford Lang.'

'And where does Inspector Conway come in?' I said.

'Sharp little ears the girl's got,' he mocked. Then: 'Conway will enter on his cue all right.' And left it at that. I was making very little headway trying to figure what it was all in aid of when the taxi drew up outside the Magnifique.

Edwin Gale was waiting by the Reception Office and his face lit up when he saw us. He came forward quickly the smoke from his cigar made us think he looked like a steamer puffing on its way.

'I can't thank you enough,' he beamed at Mr. Brett as he took the Borgia Memoirs from his reverent hands. 'Oh,' he said suddenly, 'the remainder of your fee.' He drew out a cheque from his pocket. 'All right for you?' he asked, half humorously. 'Afraid I haven't the requisite cash on me.'

Mr. Brett's smile was not so humorous

I thought. But he nodded and took the cheque all right. The other was continuing: 'And I really am most grateful to you. You've done me a very great service. Shall we go up to Mr. Lang's suite? He's awaiting this — ' he patted the book fondly — 'with keen anticipation. If you'd care to join us in a little drink — ?'

'We're right with you,' Mr. Brett said with alacrity.

In the lift Mr. Gale burbled away about his old book, pointing out to me its travel-stained appearance and yellow faded pages.

'Yes, it's had a chequered history. Drifted round Europe over four hundred years. After Borgia's death in — when was it? — in 1507 it fell into the hands of a Castillian nobleman — his name escapes me for the moment. Remained with his family a long time. Then it was stolen, I believe. Found its way to Paris. Later smuggled to this country — and even then its adventures weren't ended.' He smiled, flipping the pages and pointed out an extract for me to read. 'Interesting bit,' he said,

I obliged politely, but, could hardly make out the words, they were so faint . . . ''Now I am approaching the third year of durance within these imprisoning walls . . .'' I read; the rest was all blurred. I picked out some more further down the page . . . ''the remembrance of days Caesar Borgia was the holder of the keys to my subjects' freedom and arbiter of their fate still makes most bitter my present circumstance . . .''

The lift stopped, saving me from bothering any more over it, and we followed Mr. Gale down the luxuriously carpeted corridor.

'Yes, I guess the volume certainly lives up to your description,' Clifford Lang was saying as he concluded his inspection of the book. 'It's a rare prize.'

We were in the tall American's suite and I was clutching a gin-and-something in an atmosphere of cordial harmony. Mr. Gale was beaming all over the place, the other was quietly friendly and obviously entranced with the idea of paying over a cosy five thousand quid for the mouldy Memoirs of Mrs. Borgia's boy. I glanced at Mr. Brett, who was standing somewhat aloof busily tucking himself outside his second large scotch. I seemed to detect a sardonic quirk at the corners of his mouth, which wasn't quite in key with the pervading geniality, but maybe it was merely a fly in his drink.

Edwin Gale was saying to the American: 'It is an interesting relic, and I must say I feel a wrench letting it go.' His expression was quite rueful. I smiled at him sympathetically.

'Perhaps Mr. Lang's cash compensation will ease the pangs of parting,' I offered brightly.

Both he and the other laughed and Mr. Gale burbled, 'It'll be something to console me. All the same — ' and he gave the book an affectionate farewell pat — 'it's going a long, long way, away.'

Mr. Brett moved in and said over the rim of his glass:

'If you're finding it too heartbreaking, we might arrange for the journey to be cancelled.'

There was an edge to his voice, which made me look at him quickly. After a moment's silence I heard Edwin Gale say: 'I don't get you.' And suddenly the atmosphere of the room changed. There was a chill menace in the air.

Mr. Brett carefully gulped off the rest of his drink then said: 'Maybe my friend Inspector Conway will make my meaning clearer.'

The other's jaw dropped, then his eyes narrowed to slits of fury.

'Police? What the hell are you driving at?'

Mr. Brett spoke casually to Clifford Lang. 'Go ahead, call the Inspector in.'

'You bet,' said the American with enthusiasm and sprang to the door connecting with the bedroom, throwing it wide. Inspector Conway stood framed in the doorway, formidably backed up by another plain-clothes man behind him. 'Come right on in, Inspector,' went on Lang — unnecessarily; both men were already bearing down on a stupefied Mr. Gale. 'I guess you've heard all you need.'

Edwin Gale, on being formally charged with attempting to obtain money by false pretences, put up quite a good show of bluster and protest at first. In the end, however, he went quietly.

'Yes,' mused Mr. Brett through a cloud of cigarette-smoke some time later, 'he did a pretty convincing job. All that act about the book being pinched, and hiring me to recover it from Spencer — '

'Spencer was in it, too?' I said.

Mr. Brett nodded. 'Up to the neck. He'll have been picked up by now.'

'All with the idea of hoodwinking the American?'

'He was afraid if Lang had it in his possession too long he'd discover it was a phoney. Fixing me to bring it along like that just before he sailed gave him little chance to examine it thoroughly and at the same time coloured the whole thing an authentic shade.'

'He certainly put plenty of cunning into the job,' I said. 'And the trouble he must have taken in faking up the so-called Secret Memoirs — '

Mr. Brett grinned, thinly. 'Imagine ruining the entire artistic effect by one unpardonable error.'

'It looked genuine enough to me,' I

said. 'But you tell,' smiling at him sweetly.

'He wrote it in *English*.'

I closed my eyes in sheer mortification. 'Right under my nose,' I muttered, 'and I never saw it. Of course, *Caesar Borgia was Italian*.'

Mr. Brett, looking exceedingly smug, went on, 'Matter of fact, I had a hunch about Gale from the word go. That's what took me to Scotland Yard, to check his fingerprints I'd got on some of the money he paid me. He had a record all right. I tipped-off Conway this evening, he got onto Lang — '

I'd stopped listening. I'd been reminded of something that ought to wipe that infuriating smugness off his face like a sponge. I said: 'Pity you let him get away with paying the rest of your fee by cheque. Not much use to you now is it, Mr. Brett?'

He merely looked more sardonic than ever.

'I'll try to manage with the five hundred quid which you may recall I was supposed to pay Spencer for the book,' he said, patting his pocket, which crackled

with the musical sound of crisp bank-
notes. 'Somehow I neglected to return
these to my client.'

He sighed unconvincingly.

'A trifle forgetful of me, I fear.'

THE CASE OF THE OLD AUNT

I'd noticed the girl come in with the man, but hadn't paid much attention, except to think idly she was very young and pretty in a pink and white fragile sort of way, and the character she was with looked somehow wrong for her. She was attractive and nice-looking enough at first glance but a second view didn't register so well. In my job as secretary to Mr. Brett you learn automatically to look at people a second time, and though you can't always go by faces, of course, there are certain features that can be a warning signal if you know how to interpret them. For instance there was a hardness in this man's eyes, a rapaciousness about his mouth which told you: watch out.

It was this contrast between the two, plus the fact they sat at a table just across from mine that drew my attention to them in the first place. But as at the time I was doing all right by a late meal and not giving a thought to my figure when the waiter brought me some more sauté potatoes, I hadn't given them more than that passing thought. I'd just left the office after a really tough day, with dear, lovable Mr. Brett (how I wish sometimes he'd throw a cigarette-stub off a tall, tall building and forget to let go) at his most sardonic and infuriating, and was tired and hungry.

I'd just finished my coffee, paid the bill and was relaxing with a cigarette when the girl across the way suddenly got up from her table. The man said something, seemed to look as if he was trying to pacify her and persuade her to take it easy, but she shook her head, gathered up her things. She was leaving. I was watching the little scene with vague interest, wondering what it was all about. As the girl was about to pass me she gave me a glance. With a sudden shock I saw the intense unhappiness in her eyes. Frightened too, she was, I got that. And something else. In a fleeting second before she'd passed, that look of misery and fear gave place to a sudden desperate entreaty. As if she'd appealed to me for help. It shook me a little and I stared after her, asking myself if I'd just imagined it and wondering why she'd picked on me and what could I do about it anyway.

She was gone. The man, who'd hastily settled with a chagrined waiter, left with the untasted fish course on his hands, hurried past my table in wake of the girl. For a moment I sat there, tapping the ash off my cigarette. It was none of my business, poking my nose into it would get me precisely nowhere at all. Think me a soft-hearted dope if you like, but I couldn't get over that kid's look. It haunted me. She was badly scared, and unhappy, in need of help. Besides I was curious. Maybe it was that decided me. I got moving.

The man was handing the girl into a taxi as I came out onto the street. I caught a phrase of something he said to her: 'All right, all *right*, I won't talk about that any more. Just let me see you home — '

As they drove off, the taxi I'd halted slid to the kerb. I said:

'Tail that one in front. If you lose it I'll break your neck.'

I was smiling as I said it, of course. He was a burly figure behind the wheel and he grinned back at me appraisingly.

'Wouldn't mind a wrestle with you, lady.'

I gave him my icy stare and he chuckled as he slammed the door after me and stepped on it.

The taxi ahead turned off Sloane Street and drew up before one of those small houses with a big rental. My driver pulled up unobtrusively on the other side of the road and I watched the girl followed by the man pause outside the front door. While she dug in her handbag for the key the man did all the talking. He still seemed to be trying to calm her. She found her key, said something to him that looked like a curt goodnight and the door closed on her. The man went back to the taxi. He was just about to get in when he suddenly swung round and stared at the house as if he'd never seen it before. Then he got into the taxi and it moved on.

Well, if I was going to satisfy my

curiosity about it all I'd have to work fast and within a few moments I had a finger on the doorbell of the small house. I just hoped the girl herself would answer it, because I hadn't the faintest idea who she was and if a servant or someone answered it'd be a bit tricky for me. However, my luck was in. It was she who stood framed in the doorway. I saw how slim and young she was and tired-looking. She recognized me first look and gasped, her hand to her throat.

I smiled at her. 'I hope it's not little Miss Butt-in,' I said. 'Or that my imagination's been playing me up. But back in that restaurant I had an idea you weren't all that glad to be alive. Had a hunch, too, when you passed me on your way out you sort of threw me an SOS. I sometimes play my hunches and so — well — here I am.'

I realized I was talking exactly like Mr. Brett and I gave a little smile of amusement to myself at the thought. She was saying in a whisper:

'I don't know what did make me look at you like that — I suppose I was so

— so desperate and you seemed to have a — '

'A nice kind face,' I finished for her.

'You're very attractive,' she said. 'But there's something more than that about, you. It's in your eyes, I think, a sort of warm-hearted worldliness made me impulsively appeal to you.'

Her voice trailed off. It was all very cosy the things she'd been telling me and I fairly warmed towards her. It was nice to know, too, I hadn't made a fool of myself. I might have been all wrong about that look she'd given me. Then an idea struck me and I shot her a sharp glance. Was it all on the level? Was it some sort of plant? But I told myself as I surveyed her there could be nothing phoney about the kid. It just wasn't there. Reassured on that score I said:

'Well, what are we going to do about it?'

'About what?'

'About what's on your mind.'

'Oh.'

There was a moment of silence. I said: 'Are you in a jam or aren't you?'

'Yes,' she said slowly.

'D'you want me to help you or don't you?'

'I — I — ' she broke off. Then: 'You shouldn't have come after me. I'm sorry I behaved as I did. There's nothing you can do. Not really.'

I eyed her. I wondered if she was trying to tell me politely she'd decided on second thoughts it was something that didn't — couldn't — concern me. I shrugged. 'Right, my dear. If you're sure. Only it could be that you were right to pick on me. Maybe I'm your Fairy Godmother who could put everything tidy for you.'

She looked at me and said hesitantly: 'Who are you?'

I had nothing to lose by telling her. When I added with elaborate casualness I was secretary to a private detective she stared at me with sudden interest. 'A private detective?'

'Martin Brett,' I nodded. 'You may have heard of him.'

She shook her head and I decided maybe she wasn't the type who would have heard of Mr. Brett. After a little pause she said slowly: 'Would you care to come in for a minute?'

This was a bit of a change from her a minute ago wanting me on my way and I said, 'Why — think my magic wand might come in handy after all?'

'I think you've given me an idea,' she said and there seemed to be something ticking over at the back of her mind. A little while later found me in a quiet, nicely-furnished sitting-room with coffee and a cigarette listening to her story. The coffee was delicious and if the story wasn't the most original and intriguing I'd ever listened to I managed to fasten my interest on it. It went like this:

The kid's name was Diana Marsh; parents abroad, she was in the house alone except for an ancient housekeeper. Engaged to be married to a young man who sounded a prize mug but she was crazy over him so that was that. The character lived with a rich old aunt, his only relative, who supplied him with an allowance and on her death quite a slab of dough would come his way. Miss

Christine Rowland her name is and the old girl dotes on him. Only fly in the cream, boy was gambling fool and one thing that sends Aunt Christine off the handle is gambling. The boy had been involved in trouble at his university resulting in premature departure from seat of learning and warning from Auntie he's got to lose his taste for games of chance pronto or he can say adios to his allowance and she'll will her dough to cats' home or words to that effect.

Well, I didn't have to be exactly psychic to guess what was coming next. The boy continues gambling, gets mixed up with bunch of playmates and pretty soon is in treacle again up to his eyes. The man he owes most to is an egg named Victor Norris. He's the one I'd seen her with in the restaurant. He wants his money and when the boy says he can't pay Norris hints maybe the aunt has some jewellery tucked away which she'd never miss.

'Of course, Tony' (boy's name is Tony Rowland) 'was horrified and refused,' the girl said.

I said: 'So Norris says all right, only pay

up by a certain date or I go to your aunt?'

She gave me a little look as if surprised I could guess so much, then nodded. 'Tony is desperate. There's no one to whom he can turn.'

'How much does he owe?'

'Twelve thousand pounds.'

I whistled. Money like that doesn't grow on trees. Young Tony was certainly in a spot all right. I said, still sounding like Mr. Brett I think to myself, 'And where exactly do you figure in this?'

'I got in touch with Norris. I thought I might persuade him to give Tony time, a chance in which to pay. Not to ruin him.'

'And — ?'

'You saw us together tonight. His answer was I should persuade Tony to get the jewellery. He argued they would be Tony's one day anyway, why shouldn't he have them now, when they'll be most use to him.' Suddenly she broke down and cried like a baby. 'Oh, it's horrible,' she moaned. 'I know Tony's weak and foolish — but once we were married he would have settled down. I'd have made him pull himself together — but if his aunt throws him out, it'll be the finish of him. We shan't be able to marry and he'll go from bad to worse — '

I watched her crumpling her handkerchief into a ball. 'I thought I'd given you an idea?' I reminded her.

She looked up at me and blew her nose. 'It was — it was just clutching at a straw,' she shook her head. 'I thought perhaps your Mr. Brett might — might be able to do something. But I don't see how he could.'

I frowned a little. Frankly I didn't see what Mr. Brett could do, either. It wasn't the sort of case he'd take on, and he certainly wouldn't do it just to please me. On the other hand — I gave a little cough, and said: 'Er — well, I could ask Mr. Brett. Only thing is the question of his fee — he works on a strictly business basis — ' I mumbled on feeling somewhat hot under the collar as I tried to apologize for Mr. Brett's cold cash calculating-machine that served in place of his heart.

She said at once: 'I've a little money. Of course, I'd expect to pay his fee — if he could save Tony.'

'If he can't, no one else can,' I said with conviction. 'And he'll tell you frankly yes or no. If it's yes, your worry is over.'

Her face brightened and I went on: 'Be at the office eleven tomorrow morning. I'll take you into him,' and I gave her the address.

I told Mr. Brett all about it after I had taken in his mail the next morning. He'd come in rather earlier than usual as a matter of fact, interrupting my routine reading of the newspapers, and was looking more saturnine than ever. I decided privately getting up early didn't suit him. He didn't say a word while I told him how I'd first of all noticed Diana Marsh and the man at the restaurant, then followed their taxi and had learned the girl's story. He just balanced himself in his chair with his feet inevitably on the desk and stared through the cigarette smoke at the ceiling. Even when I ended up with: 'Well I hope you're pleased I've booked a client for you — I think she's got enough for your fee anyway,' he didn't look in the least bit interested.

He murmured, still staring at the

ceiling: 'You say you fixed her to see me at eleven?'

'Yes, Mr. Brett.'

He was silent for a moment. Then: 'Might as well take a view of your little innocent, I suppose.'

Something in his voice made me ask slowly: 'You think she was merely leading me up the garden?' And I recalled the sudden thought I'd had last night that maybe Diana Marsh wasn't all she made out to be.

'I have a suspicious nature,' he said through a puff of cigarette smoke, 'and believe everyone's a liar until I find out the truth.' He yawned elaborately. 'But obviously, my Gorgeous Girl Gumshoe,' he went on sardonically, 'you haven't read this morning's papers.' And while I was burning up with fury at his gratuitously familiar tone he swung his feet to the floor and pushed a newspaper across to me. 'Front page,' he said. 'Stop Press.'

I looked where he indicated and could hardly credit my peepers. But there it was all right, in black and white:

'ELDERLY SPINSTER
FOUND DEAD

In the early hours of the morning Miss Christine Rowland was found dead at her house in Park Square, W.1., in suspicious circumstances. Woman's nephew, Anthony Rowland, discovered the body and at once notified the police. It is understood Scotland Yard are making enquiries with regard to the tragedy.'

I gaped at Mr. Brett over the newspaper and he leered back at me.

'What price your innocent friend now?'

'But Mr. Brett,' I protested, 'what makes you think she had anything to do with this?'

He shrugged. "Maybe no, maybe yes. Who can tell? She'd have lost a potential rich hubby if Auntie had kicked Rowland out, don't forget. Now she's got him plus legacy safely hooked and Norris can go fly a kite.'

I shook my head slowly. 'She was desperately scared of Norris when I saw her, of that I'm positive. And why should she fix herself up in murder *after* she'd discovered who I was and agreed to come and see you?' I went on: 'Besides, she just isn't the sort who could do anything like that.'

'Maybe she's merely an accessory before or after the fact,' he conceded. Which was generous of him, I thought, in a repulsive kind of way.

I said thoughtfully: 'My bet would be the boy could have done it — '

The phone jangled into life. Mr. Brett grinned at it. 'My bet would be it's the Marsh piece cancelling her appointment,' he murmured.

He was right about it being her, but she didn't want to cancel her appointment exactly. She wanted to see Mr. Brett more urgently than ever. When was the earliest he could manage it?

'I've seen the papers,' I told her gently. 'What a terrible shock for you — '

'Worse still has happened,' she cut in, her voice hitting a hysterical note. 'Tony — *they suspect Tony* — '

She babbled on about how the police had questioned him, warned him not to leave the house, and he was left in dread suspense, convinced his arrest on charge of murdering his aunt was imminent. 'He's innocent — he's innocent, Mr. Brett can prove it, I know — I must see him as soon as possible — '

'If you'll hold on, I'll ask Mr. Brett if he can be available earlier,' I said. I covered the receiver and raised a questioning eyebrow at Mr. Brett.

'I'll see her when she gets here,' he said succinctly and put his feet on the desk again. I gave the girl his message and she said she'd be along in twenty minutes. When I'd hung up Mr. Brett said: 'Get me Conway.' As I got through to Scotland Yard he added: 'Better listen-in, take notes.'

Detective-Inspector Conway came on the line and I went into my office to listen to him and Mr. Brett on my extension. The C.I.D. man was saying with his typically heavy-handed humour: 'Who's your client in this case, Brett? Don't tell me it's the woman's nephew.'

'I don't tell you,' said Mr. Brett.

'No, I've never known you to be on the

wrong horse yet.'

'There's always a first time,' Mr. Brett said agreeably. Then: 'So you don't fancy Rowland's chances?'

'Frankly, not much.'

'Since you mention being frank, what d'you know?'

'He found his aunt in her bedroom at one-thirty this morning with her head dented. Been awakened by some noise he said. Signs of a struggle and her jewellery — family heirloom stuff — gone. He calls the doctor — which is a waste of time, she was dead — and us. That's *his* story. Well, it's all right, of course — only he's the sole heir and the old girl didn't do herself in, Admittedly it seemed possible it could have been an outside job — fact of the jewellery being pinched for one thing — '

'I was thinking the theft doesn't fit in with the theory Rowland bumped off Auntie to get his hooks on the legacy a bit quicker.'

'No, but the boy's no fool. Our idea is he shifted the stuff deliberately to throw suspicion on someone outside.'

'You sound pretty definite about his guilt.'

'We've had a tip-off which makes it look even more definite. It appears Rowland who's a bit of a play-boy type was up to the neck in gambling debts and if his aunt had found out she'd have disowned him.'

'Who tipped you that information?'

'Some woman phoned. Wouldn't give her name. It's my belief she knew something all right.'

'On the other hand,' Mr. Brett said after a moment, 'was there any evidence to show it could have been an outside job?'

'Thought you said Rowland isn't your client?' Conway chuckled meaningfully.

'I'm working for his girlfriend,' Mr. Brett said, adding: 'I think.'

'Well, bedroom's on first floor overlooking a small garden back of the house. Balcony outside which could be fairly easily reached from the garden, admittedly. Rowland stated the window opening onto the balcony was in fact ajar when he entered the bedroom. But the aunt may have left it open, or he may have opened it to give the impression someone had entered and exited that way. But there were no signs the window'd been forced, no traces whatsoever on the balcony or in the garden anyone had come or gone that way.' And the Detective-Inspector bit out this point with emphasis.

'Doesn't look as if Rowland's as smart as you make him out,' Mr. Brett said slowly. 'You'd think he'd have thought of that, wouldn't you?' And I caught a slightly sardonic edge to his tone.

'You know the saying: The criminal always makes a mistake,' Conway chortled back. 'Wouldn't be criminals if they didn't.'

'What would they be — detective-inspectors?'

But I think Conway missed the finer subtlety of that remark. He only just guffawed. Followed a little heavy-handed badinage from the C.I.D. man and Mr. Brett rang off.

A few minutes later Diana Marsh turned up. She looked pretty grim and I felt genuinely sorry for her, knowing as I did that her boyfriend seemed to be for it. Mr. Brett glowered morosely out of the window as if he was expecting it to pour with rain all the time she talked to him. The only time he showed any interest in what she had to say was when she asked him about his fee. She said Tony knew she was coming to see him, she was to spare no money if it would help tear down the terrible shadow that hung over him. Whether Mr. Brett's sudden interest lay in the prospect of handling a nice slice of dough, or whether he was commenting privately (as I was) on young Rowland's readiness with his dead aunt's money before it had actually been made over to him, I wouldn't know. Not that the poor young devil could be blamed for acting like that anyway.

Diana Marsh added nothing of importance to Mr. Brett's knowledge of the set-up already learned from Inspector Conway and from me. And he didn't appear to be in the least bit stirred by her pathetic helplessness, her desperate appeal for help. He ended the interview with typical brusqueness.

'I'll handle the case. It'll make a change to take on a job with all the cards stacked against me — my secretary will fix the fee.'

After she'd gone I went back into his office. He was on his way out. He glanced at his wristwatch and grinned at me. 'Just popping out for a quick one,' he said. At the door he turned. 'By the way you know Victor Norris's address?'

I nodded. I'd made a note of it when the Marsh girl mentioned it earlier. It was a flat in a block off Tottenham Court Road. Mr. Brett said, 'Meet me outside the place in an hour's time.'

I stared at him a little puzzled. 'What d'you think he'll know?' I said. And added: 'If he's at home to tell you.'

'He'll probably be out,' he murmured and I gave him a sharp look. But his expression was enigmatic. The door closed after him and I stood frowning to myself as his footsteps faded along the passage.

An hour later found me waiting by the entrance to the flats. It was a large barn of a building and as I paced up and down I caught glimpses of an over-decorated vestibule beyond the swing-doors. Mr. Brett arrived in a few minutes and we went up in the self-operated lift.

'I suppose you think I've spent the entire time since I left you propping up a bar?' he jeered at me.

I looked at him wide-eyed. 'Frankly, Mr. Brett,' I said, 'I hadn't given it a thought. I expect I was too busy. You know,' I added sweetly, 'office routine still operates even when you're out.'

But the sting didn't seem to penetrate. He said, with elaborate casualness: 'In case you're interested, I spent a while taking a look at a house in Park Square.'

'See Tony Rowland?' I asked him.

He shook his head. 'Just the outside of the house,' he said and contemplated the tip of his cigarette. The lift stopped at the fourth floor and we got out. As Mr. Brett pressed a long finger against the bell push of Victor Norris's flat, I said quickly: 'Suppose he *is* in?'

'That's why I brought you along,' he said blandly. 'To dazzle him with your glamorous charms, maybe put him off his guard at the crucial moment.'

He grinned at me sardonically but I wasn't amused. I eyed him coldly. I resented his bright idea he'd been getting lately I could be dragged round as a sort of decoy duck. Then we heard someone on the other side of the door and he hissed mockingly in my ear: 'Don't forget to waggle your eyelashes at him, Gorgeous — I'm told it knocks 'em flat.'

But it was a woman who faced us. A tough-looking redhead obviously didn't care for our appearances one little bit. But she risked her displeasure to ogle Mr. Brett coyly.

'What d'you want — tall, dark and not unhandsome?' she said from the side of her mouth. Mr. Brett blew a cloud of cigarette smoke in her dial in a most ungentlemanly way.

'It definitely wouldn't be you,' he muttered and while the redhead was getting the smoke out of her eyes he'd pushed past her. I stuck close to him as I could without actually getting under his coat. The tiny hall led to a lounge and Victor Norris faced us scowling all over his face at us.

'What's-the-big-idea-who-the-hell-are-you-get-out,' he rasped all in one vehement mouthful.

Unabashed, Mr. Brett said: 'The big idea is I'm a private detective hired by a certain Miss Diana Marsh. And believe me I'll get out just as soon as you've answered one or two questions.' He went on with smooth affability: 'The name's Brett, you're Victor Norris, correct me if I'm wrong.'

Norris was looking past us, and I turned to see the redhead behind us. He said to her: 'All right, I'll see you later. Meet me at the club for lunch.'

The woman stood there for a moment, then went and a moment later the front door slammed.

'A friend of mine,' Norris said.

'Don't apologize,' Mr. Brett murmured, and the other shot a nasty look at him. He turned to stare at me as if he was wondering if he'd seen me before. I let him wonder and he said to Mr. Brett:

'What's Diana Marsh got to do with me?'

'Not a thing — beyond the fact you advised her if young Rowland didn't pinch his aunt's jewellery it'd be too bad for him.'

'That's a damned lie.'

Mr. Brett shrugged. 'I see it embarrassed you, so let's talk about something else. About, for instance, your — er — friend just departed.' He paused to tap the ash off his cigarette. 'This morning someone phoned Scotland Yard, tipped them off about Rowland being neck-deep in debt and that he would benefit more than somewhat by his aunt's will. You get the implication?'

Norris looked at him coldly. 'I thought you would,' Mr. Brett purred. 'The caller was a woman, and the cops checked the call-box she used. Naturally she'd gone, but they found a strand of hair caught in the receiver. It was red hair.' And he drew slowly at his cigarette.

I saw a shadow of uneasiness flicker across the other's face as I wondered how Mr. Brett had got hold of this tasty morsel of information. Norris said: 'My friend's not the only red-haired woman who's ever used a phone-box — if that's what you're getting at.'

Mr. Brett permitted a mirthless smile to quirk the corners of his mouth. 'I'm glad you're keeping in step with me. But maybe you'll agree it's too coincidental to be true that the mysterious redhead also knew something not exactly common knowledge concerning Rowland? Knowledge, which for example you could have imparted to her.'

The silence was pretty tense.

Then Norris drew a deep breath. 'You're smart at putting two and two together, aren't you?'

'I went to school,' Mr. Brett said.

'Okay,' the other said. 'I did get her to make that anonymous call. When I read about Rowland's aunt this morning, I felt in my bones he'd done it. Thought the police might like to know a few facts about that nasty piece of work her nephew. The twister owed me twelve thousand quid and told me I could whistle for it.' He added hurriedly, 'That

226

yarn that I tried to get him to knock off the woman's bric-a-brac is laughable, of course.'

It didn't seem to be amusing Mr. Brett. He said quietly: 'If I were to mention I know the robbery was in fact an outside job, that Rowland is in the clear, what would you say?'

The other laughed, not a very nice laugh. 'I'd say where's the proof?'

'On the dining room window which faces the street. Fresh marks indicating the catch was forced. The intruder got in, and no doubt out, that way. He made a cunning job of it. Leaving the bedroom window open with no scratch or foot-marks on the balcony or in the garden would, he calculated, set the police figuring Rowland had made a futile attempt to shift suspicion onto someone breaking in from the garden. He figured no one would tumble to the marks on the dining room window through which *he* had popped.' He smiled thinly. 'He was right,' he went on easily, 'almost. No one did tumble to it — except me,'

Norris shifted his neck in his collar.

'Pretty neat of you,' he said coolly. 'Though it seems to me Rowland still might be an accomplice of this other whoever-he-is. He could have been working on the inside.'

'If he was,' Mr. Brett purred, 'why didn't he make it easier for his pal to get in? Instead of leaving him to fiddle with the window-latch and risk being spotted by a passing cop?''

'Got it all parceled up haven't you?' the other sneered. Then he said with a brisk heartiness: 'Well, thanks very much for showing me the way a sleuth's mind works. It's been very interesting, but you'll have to excuse me now.'

Mr. Brett's only move was to stub out his cigarette. I watched him crush it to shreds in the ashtray and waited for what was coming next, my mind a little bit foggy, hoping we'd get out without any ugly scene. Victor Norris was saying, 'Unless there's anything more you'd like to know from me?' And added: 'Afraid I can't confess to being your mystery man, if that's what you're hoping.' He laughed, again not very nicely. 'I'm not the type who can scheme things out like that. Besides, I've got one of those cast-iron alibis you sometimes hear about.'

Mr. Brett glanced at him. 'Is that so?'

The other nodded emphatlcally. 'I was right here in this dinky little flat at half-past one this morning, entertaining friends.'

'The party including our red-haired acquaintance?' Mr. Brett asked slowly.

Norris hesitated. Then: 'Yes, she was here, and a couple from a flat in this building. So there you are.'

'Thanks for the information.' And Mr. Brett turned to me with a nod indicating we were moving. At the door he paused, lit a fresh cigarette and observed: 'Hope you won't be late for your luncheon engagement.'

In the lift I said: 'What now, Mr. Brett? Or am I too young to know?'

He grinned at me sardonically. 'It'll be a fairly old-fashioned routine,' he said. 'While Victor Norris is hurriedly packing we call the police who'll just hang around and pick him up when he comes out. The betting is Auntie's — er — bric-a-brac

229

will be wrapped up in his shirts and socks.'

Mr. Brett was right, of course. The police collared Norris, suitcase and all, about half-an-hour later as he was stepping into a taxi. He fought like a demon, but it got him nowhere at all, at least nowhere he wanted to go to. Mr. Brett was wrong about the shirts and socks though. Aunt Christine's jewellery was wrapped in a pair of pale blue pyjamas. But as he said later when I chided him gently about it:

'It wasn't such a whale of a mistake as he made when he yapped about being at his flat at one-thirty yesterday morning.'

'That was when the murder took place?'

'Exactly. But how did *Norris* know that? It wasn't mentioned in the newspaper report and nobody could have told him. *Yet he'd carefully built up an alibi for the very time the murder was committed.* Which means he must have known too much about it than was good for him.'

He chuckled, he was in an almost

humanly good humour — he'd got a
drink in his hand. I said: 'What's so
funny?'

'I was thinking about the redhead.'

I regarded him quizzically. 'Would you
care for me to get myself up in a henna
shampoo and start leaving bits of my hair
all over the office phones?'

He chuckled again. 'The red hair
caught in the call-box phone came out of
my head,' he said. 'With the stuff about
the cops checking up where she'd phoned
from and the rest. *That's* what's so
funny.'

THE CASE OF THE
GIRL IN THE
CALL BOX

It was latish, Mr. Brett's office was heavy with the grey-blue haze from the endless succession of cigarettes he'd been smoking, and I was just about to suggest to him I opened the window and let in a gulp of fresh air when the phone on his desk jangled.

'Leave it,' Mr. Brett growled as I moved forward to grab the receiver.

I looked at him and shrugged. 'Supposing it's someone threatened with having their throat cut?' I murmured brightly as the burr-burr continued.

'Anyone who chooses this time of night for it deserves to get their throat cut,' he snapped irritably. 'Besides, I've had enough of this racket for one day.'

That suited me, too; I was fed up with work and wanted to get home, but after all business was business and even if the caller was ringing well after office hours I didn't like leaving whoever it was unanswered. Still, if Mr. Brett wasn't worrying, why should I work myself up into a nervous breakdown over it?

The phone went on ringing while we pretended not to hear it and went on clearing up the job we had on hand. It was in fact only the routine business concerning a case Mr. Brett had recently taken care of for an insurance company, which ordinarily we'd have carried over to the following day. Only the detailed report being already overdue for delivery to the firm in question, I'd managed to persuade Mr. Brett it really should be finished and done with even if it meant an hour or two late at the office.

The phone continued to jangle. Whoever it was thought they needed Mr. Brett's help seemed to be in a pretty persistent frame of mind about it. Mr. Brett scowled at the instrument and finally gave me the nod. As I reached for the darned thing he told me:

'Tell 'em I've taken a trip to Tanganyika.'

'Mr. Martin Brett's office,' I said,

trying to convey by my tone that it was through some supreme miracle the phone *was* being answered. A girl's voice came over the wire, and she sounded in a panic all right.

'I prayed someone might be there,' she said, all choked and breathless. 'I know it's late, but if Mr. Brett — '

'I'm afraid Mr. Brett — ' I began with the automatically weary note well laid on. But she cut in.

'Oh, I'm sure he's gone — but if you could please tell me where I could find him — ' Oh, yes, she was persistent, but there was such entreaty behind her words, I somehow felt it wasn't a pet Peke she'd lost in the park, or her paste-earring she'd dropped on a bus.

'If you could give me some idea,' I said glibly, 'perhaps I could help you?'

Out of the corner of my eye I caught Mr. Brett's yawn.

'You're very kind,' the girl said, and it struck me it was a nice voice, young but with a certain timbre to it that aroused my sympathy. 'But I don't think anyone but Mr. Brett could *really* do anything.

237

You — you see, it's *murder*!'

'Murder!' I said, shooting a look across at Mr. Brett. 'Who's murdered who?'

'It's Miss Dalby who's been — ' She broke off and went on, 'I don't know who did it. Oh, please, where can I find Mr. Brett? I'm so frightened they'll say it was I — '

'Why should they — ?' I began, but she was sobbing brokenly.

'You don't understand! You don't understand — please tell me where Mr. Brett is, I beg you — '

Well, this was all grim stuff to be hearing and I placed my hand over the receiver and told Mr. Brett: 'Some young woman mixed up in a murder or something. Wants you to help her out.'

He tapped the end off his cigarette negligently. 'I didn't hear you tell her I'd gone to Pago-Pago,' he said.

The voice over the wire was burbling in my ear. I couldn't catch all of it, but I got something about: 'I'll kill myself — It's driving me out of my mi — I'll commit suicide —

I said to him, 'She sounds the young

hysterical type. Maybe if you spoke to
her — '

'The young hysterical type is my
favourite kind of client,' he jeered. Then:
'Where's she talking from?' he said, but
without the slightest interest.

I asked the girl.

'From a phone-box by Regent's Park. I
daren't — I *can't* go back to the flat.'

'Hold on,' I said, 'I'll see if I can find
out where Mr. Brett may be.'

'She's at a call-box,' I said to Mr. Brett,
muffling the phone again. 'Regent's Park
way. She really sounds in a jam.'

He surveyed me through a cloud of
cigarette smoke. 'What d'you think I
should do about it, Gorgeous?'

I flashed back icily: 'Shall I ask her how
much money she's got to spend?'

He stared at me his eyes widening.
'Anyone'd think I'm interested only in
getting my fee out of people,' he purred.

I didn't make the obvious comeback, it
wasn't worth it, besides I was frankly
perturbed about the girl at the other end
of the phone. I had the idea she was
pretty desperate and it mightn't be so

good for the Martin Brett office if we brushed her off and left her to go jump off a very high building or take an overdose of sleeping tablets. I said into the phone:

'I'm just checking up where Mr. Brett's gone to — it's possible he's coming back presently, as it happens — ' Mr. Brett gave me a sour grimace, but I didn't let it bother me — 'meantime, if you could tell me a bit more about yourself?'

'Oh, thank you. Thank you so much — ' she said fervently. 'My name's Mary Harcourt. I'm secretary-companion — or *was* — to Miss Dalby — '

While she was talking I said across to Mr. Brett again:

'She's secretary-companion to one of those well-off spinsters. Might be something in it for you after all.' And smiled at him sweetly.

He tried not to look suddenly interested but didn't succeed too well. 'Maybe I *could* have just got back from wherever I've been,' he suggested, grinning sardonically.

I said to the girl quickly:

'Hold on a moment, I think I hear Mr. Brett coming in — '

'How wonderful — !'

'Yes,' I went on after an appropriate pause. 'It *is* him. Just wait please, while I have a word with him.' I put down the receiver and looked at Mr. Brett questioningly.

'Ask her where we can pick her up,' he muttered in a low voice. 'Tell her to wait there. I'll be along as soon as possible.'

'Yes, Mr. Brett.'

The girl said she'd wait outside the call-box, giving me exact directions where it was and I told her to stick around until we showed up. She was still babbling her gratitude at me when I hung up.

In the taxi on the way Mr. Brett observed, with a certain moroseness: 'Matter of fact, if it's the well-off spinster who's been bumped off she *won't* be handing out the fee.'

'Maybe she'll have left it all to the secretary, so you'll be able to send her the bill,' I said, trying to cheer him up.

His long face limned in the glow of his cigarette was bitter as he turned to me.

'Rich spinsters *always* leave their cash to cats' homes,' he said emphatically, 'particularly cats' homes already bulging with fat legacies. Seldom does the poor secretary-companion get a sniff at a brass farthing. It's a way rich spinsters have and something should be done about it.'

'Such as leaving their money to a fund for retired private detectives?' I said.

He said: 'I had already thought of that.'

Mr. Brett left me to pay off the taxi as we pulled up alongside the call-box while he went over to the girl who stood waiting expectantly in the pool of light from a street-lamp. As I joined him — taking a mental note of the fare to take out of the petty cash — I heard her telling him:

'She's dead, Mr. Brett.' She spoke in hurried gasps, blurting out the words as if they'd been bottled up inside her. 'I went out just now to post the letters — I do every evening, you see — and when I came back I found her — ' She broke off and her voice hit a high note of near-hysteria. 'I didn't do it — I didn't — '

He cut in: 'Try and relax. Just tell me

what happened and don't rush it. Don't rush any of it.'

She gave him a grateful look.

'Yes, Mr. Brett. Oh, thank heavens I managed to find you. I'd read about you in the newspapers and when — this happened — I rushed out. I didn't know what I was doing, then I suddenly thought of you — '

'People often do when they're in trouble,' Mr. Brett told her sardonically through a puff of cigarette smoke. Then: 'But just you say what you did after you found your — er — late employer. You took a dive, you were saying?'

'Yes. I lost my head. The way she looked. Oh, it was ghastly.' She shuddered violently, at the remembered horror. She was a thin-faced girl of about twenty-five, plainly, almost shabbily, dressed, with a crushed air about her that made her seem very pathetic. She continued: 'I rushed out of the flat — '

'Without stopping to call a doctor, or the cops?' Mr. Brett's tone as he said it was casual, almost conversational. A little too casual and I gave the girl a quick look. She'd caught that under-note in his voice and she burst out defensively:

'I daren't. You don't understand. They'll say I did it. She was always telling her friends and people — she even told the hall-porter — I hated her, that I'd be glad to see her dead.' She broke off again to add pathetically: 'Miss Dalby wasn't very nice sometimes. She was cruel — '

Mr. Brett said evenly:

'Supposing we took a look at her?'

'No,' she gasped. 'I can't — I couldn't face it — '

Mr. Brett regarded the tip of his cigarette. The girl started to cry quietly and I took her arm.

'Take it easy,' I said to her. 'It'll be all right. If you didn't harm Miss Dalby — and I'm sure you didn't — no one's going to take it out of you.'

She dabbed her eyes with a screwed-up handkerchief.

'All right,' she said. 'I'll go back.' She turned to Mr. Brett. 'I'm sorry. You must think me an hysterical fool — but — but the shock, I — '

'Couldn't we get going?' he interrupted

her, with a touch of impatience.

'It's Parkside Mansions,' she said. 'Across the road, on the corner of Regent's Crescent.'

Parkside Mansions was a small, select-looking block of flats. The glass double doors were open and Mr. Brett paused, glancing into the softly-lit entrance-hall beyond.

'Porter's on duty,' he said to the girl. 'Did he see you come out?'

She hesitated a moment then, 'No. I used the stairs, not the lift. We're only on the second floor.'

Mr. Brett nodded and we went in. The porter greeted the girl cheerily but with an expression of slight surprise. ''Ello, Miss 'Arcourt.' He turned to grin at us. He was a somewhat undersized character. Sandy-haired. About forty. I noticed although he was in uniform he'd no cap and a cigarette-stub was stuck behind his ear. As we got into the lift he glanced sympathetically at the girl.

'You seem a bit done-in, Miss, if I may say so.' And looked at me as if for confirmation.

I nodded. 'Miss Harcourt is a little seedy, but we'll take care of her.'

The man pressed the button and we whirred upwards. Again he eyed the girl with that slight air of puzzlement and said: 'I didn't notice you go out, Miss 'Arcourt.'

She began to stammer something but Mr. Brett butted in with: 'You been on duty here all night?'

'I 'ave, as a matter of fact,' came the answer, the porter's tone suggesting it wasn't any of Mr. Brett's business anyway. 'Sorry you ain't feeling up to the mark,' he said to the girl. ' 'Ope you'll feel better in the mornin'. Second floor.'

The lift stopped and we got out.

'Mr. Palmer ain't arrived yet,' the porter volunteered through the lift-gates as they slid in front of him. 'Good-night.' And pressing the button he disappeared from view.

Mr. Brett surveyed the girl.

'Palmer?'

'He's Miss Dalby's solicitor,' she explained. Her face lit up with a wan smile for a moment. 'He's an old friend of her family and very kind. I — I'd forgotten he was expected for coffee this evening, he usually looks in once or twice a month. Oh, it'll be horrible for him — '

'You lived with her alone?' Mr. Brett was saying as we moved down the short corridor.

'Yes.'

We reached a cream-coloured door and she produced a Yale key from her handbag. We followed her into the small hall. Mr. Brett gazed around him with an abstract air. On the right was a miniature hallstand holding a woman's overcoat, hat and umbrella. Beyond the hall was a door slightly ajar. The girl nodded to it.

'In — in there,' she said shakily.

Mr. Brett glanced at her. 'You left the light on,' he observed.

The light was in fact burning in the room ahead. She answered half-apologetically, 'I must have forgotten it when I rushed out.'

She looked a ghastly colour and I took her arm comfortingly. She flashed me a wan, grateful little smile.

Mr. Brett said over his shoulder as he

strode ahead into the room: 'You'd better come in, too.'

I followed the girl, who after hesitating pulled herself together and then went in. She hung back as Mr. Brett bent over the bed on which the huddled figure lay. He gave it a cursory survey. 'Smothered to death,' he murmured half to himself. He stood up and lit a cigarette. He glanced round the bedroom slowly. It was small but nicely furnished. Obviously the late Miss Dalby was cozily-off all right.

The girl started to sway a little. 'It's dreadful. Dreadful!' she moaned. Mr. Brett glanced at her, then at me and gave me a nod. I crossed quickly and grabbed her arm.

'Sit down,' I told her. 'And don't look. You don't have to.'

She parked herself on the edge of a chair and leaned back, eyes closed. I stayed near her, watching Mr. Brett. He moved suddenly to the window, at which the curtains fluttered in a draught.

'Window's open,' he said.

The Harcourt girl sat up, her eyes widening. 'That's funny,' she said. 'Miss

Dalby always closed it in the evening. When she came to bed, which was always very early, she locked her door, too.'

'That so?' Mr. Brett said over his shoulder as he leant out of the window. 'Leads to the fire escape.' He ducked his head back into the room. 'Wouldn't have been overwhelmingly tricky for someone to force the catch and pop in and out this way.'

'You mean the murderer?' she asked in a low voice.

He turned and regarded her, his face saturnine and sharpened as he rapped back: 'No, someone just dropping by to say 'good-night'.' He was looking round the room again, speculatively. He said to the girl, his eyes on a small print over by the dressing table, 'You say she always locked the door at night?'

'Yes.'

'What was she afraid of?'

'Her jewellery. She kept it here.'

He said with deceptive casualness. 'Any idea where?'

There was a slight pause. Then: 'No. Miss Dalby never told me.'

Mr. Brett examined the tip of his cigarette with absorbed attention. After a moment he went on: 'So she locked herself in. Would she open the door to you?'

'Sometimes. But she didn't like being disturbed. Most nights she used to sit in the armchair reading for a while before going to bed. Sometimes Mr. Palmer would call and see her. He looked after her business in the City and occasionally he'd come in when he'd been working late and she wanted to know about certain of her business matters. He lives nearby. He'd usually have some coffee with Miss Dalby. I'd take it in to them.'

'Correct me if I'm being crazy, but I seem to have the impression you weren't exactly devoted to your boss?'

She bit her lip. Then said firmly: 'I didn't like her, but she might have been worse. I didn't do *that* to her.' She fixed her eyes on the bed for a moment then closed them with a shiver.

Mr. Brett made no comment. He turned to me. 'Entice the porter here, will you? I'd like a word with him, then we'd better call the police,'

'Yes, Mr. Brett,' I said, and with a reassuring smile at the girl I beat it.

I was back in a few minutes with the porter who seemed suitably impressed with the horror of the tragedy. 'Pore lady, wot a terrible thing to 'ave 'appened,' he kept on saying on our way up in the lift. He was apparently deeply affected. 'One of the nicest tenants we 'ave — er — 'ad — ' he carefully corrected himself.

But as he faced Mr. Brett in the bedroom I noticed his pallor and the nervous twitch that had appeared underneath one eye. He was trembling a little also. Might mean nothing, might mean something, I thought.

'Before I call the police,' Mr. Brett was telling him, 'maybe it'd be an idea to ask you a couple of questions.'

'Suits me,' said the other promptly. 'Only thing is wot right you got? Eh?'

Mr. Brett carefully told him about his rights and the porter mouthed 'Oh' in a subdued gulp and went even paler about the gills.

'Must be an awful shock for you,' Mr.

Brett said with an oblique glance at the inert shape on the bed. He said it in an almost sympathetic tone but his eyes were sharp and narrowed.

The man nodded. "Orrible, it is,'

'You the head-porter here?'

'Yessir. Name's Horton, Albert Horton in case yer wants ter know. Everyone calls me 'Bert' naturally. I got an assistant — 'e was on duty this arternoon from midday up till tea-time.'

'You've been around since then?'

''Sright'

'Who've used the lift during that time?'

'Not many.' He pondered a moment, pulling at his lower lip. 'It was just arter I came on that I took Miss Dillon up to her flat on the third . . . Then, 'arf-an-'our later it'd be, I brings Mr. and Mrs. Fulton down from the fourth . . . Little arter six pip emm there was Mr. Bell up ter three . . . Then — ' he paused to scratch the back of his head.

'Anyway, no one *unknown* to you used the lift?'

'No one, sir.' Emphatically.

'How about the stairs?' I chimed in helpfully.

Mr. Brett regarded me with a certain sourness. 'All right, Dream Girl, I'm taking care of this.'

'Sorry, Mr. Brett — '

But he was chatting casually to Horton again. He asked him:

'You took Miss Harcourt down when she went to the post?'

''Sright.'

'And brought her back when she returned?'

The porter looked at the girl with a slight frown creasing his forehead. 'Yus,' he agreed slowly.

'But you *didn't* bring her down in the lift before she came in with us?'

'No, that's wot puzzled me — when I saw Miss 'Arcourt come in with you. I must have just popped off ter get a cigarette.'

Mr. Brett made no comment on that explanation. He merely flicked the ash off his cigarette and murmured thoughtfully: 'So you couldn't swear no one slipped up here during that time without your knowing it?'

'I suppose I couldn't swear to that. But they'd 'ave to 'ave been pretty spry. And anyway, 'ow did they get away? I'd 'ave spotted 'em coming down at least.' He shook his head with a knowing air. 'No, sir,' he said, 'I reckon it was someone in the flats done it. O' course, I ain't no detective, but that's my opinion, for what it's worth.'

'Which isn't much,' Mr. Brett told him succinctly.

Horton said, 'Oh' again and subsided.

Mr. Brett appeared to lose interest in him and he let his gaze wander round the room while he drew abstractedly at his cigarette. Horton stood uneasily first on one foot then on the other. He glanced at me, then at the Harcourt girl. Then he took the cigarette stub from behind his ear. He was about to light it when he remembered the figure on the bed and with an air of embarrassment pushed the stub behind his ear again. Mr. Brett who'd had a cigarette drooping from his mouth all the time said to him:

'Smoke if you want, Horton, it soothes the nerves.'

'Yes, sir. Thanks — I do feel a bit shaky. The shock I expect.'

'I expect so,' Mr. Brett nodded — and then suddenly jerked his head up in a tense, listening attitude.

I lent a sharp ear myself and caught the faint humming sound, which had attracted Mr. Brett's attention.

It was the lift ascending.

The noise grew louder and the porter exclaimed: 'Somebody usin' the lift now.'

There was nothing to it, of course, I mean what's so unusual about people using a lift in a block of flats? But all the same I could feel a momentary tightening of the atmosphere as that humming grew. I found myself remembering something I'd once heard about how the murderer always returns to the scene of his crime. Silly of me, I knew, because even as I gave a slight shiver it occurred to me whoever had bumped off Miss Dalby and wanted a second look would hardly dare to come back quite so openly.

Mr. Brett made me jump to it by suddenly snapping at me: 'Cut the dreamy-eyed stuff, Beautiful, and shut the door.'

I moved like a flash and, as the lift stopped at the second floor and I heard the sound of the lift gate sliding open, swiftly closed the bedroom door. Horton and the girl stared at Mr. Brett who snapped: 'Not a squeak from any of you.'

'Blimey wot's the idea — ?' began the porter but Mr. Brett bit out a warning at him.

'Shut up.'

The room was eerily silent except for the sound of the porter's somewhat asthmatic breathing, then the electric-bell cut the stillness like a knife. The Harcourt girl gave a gasp.

'It's Mr. Palmer,' she exclaimed.

'Stay where you are,' Mr. Brett's voice hissed at her.

'But — but he wants to come in,' she answered in a low voice. 'He — '

'I don't imagine he's ringing just for the hell of it,' Mr. Brett muttered. *'Keep quiet.'*

The bell rang again. And again.

Followed a long pause. Then suddenly

256

but unmistakably came the scrape of a key in the Yale lock.

'He's got a key,' whispered the girl, her voice charged with sudden apprehension. 'Mr. Palmer never had a key — '

'If you don't shut up, I'll sock you,' Mr. Brett rasped in a savage undertone.

The front door opened and closed quietly. Footsteps approached and a voice called out, a cheery, plaintive sounding baritone. 'Miss Dalby . . . '

There was a choked gasp from the girl. A pause as if the newcomer was making sure there was no reply, then the bedroom door opened and a thick-set man, slightly bald, stood framed in the doorway. He gazed first at one then another of us in what might be described as some surprise,

'Mr. Palmer!' the girl said but he didn't hear her — his eyes were suddenly fixed on the bed.

'What — what's happened?' he gulped and with a quick movement was at the bedside.

'Miss Dalby's dead,' the girl said unnecessarily.

Palmer turned to Mr. Brett questioningly.

'Must be a terrible shock to you,' Mr. Brett said, and in answer to the other's query told him who he was and what he was doing there. He remembered to include me in the introduction, too.

'This is ghastly,' the solicitor muttered. 'Ghastly.' He glanced again at the bed. 'When — when did it happen?' he asked, taking out a handkerchief and dabbing his face with it.

Mr. Brett said: 'Within the last thirty or forty minutes I'd say.'

'Suicide?'

'I think we can dismiss any idea the woman smothered herself. It would be a somewhat unusual way of bumping herself off.'

'Miss Dalby *was* slightly eccentric,' Palmer offered.

Mr. Brett said gently through a puff of cigarette smoke. 'Not all that eccentric.'

The other looked at him, frowning. 'You mean it's murder?'

Mr. Brett nodded,

'Oughtn't the police to be called in?

Whoever did this dreadful thing isn't going to get away with it. I mean,' he went on, bringing a touch of apology to his tone, 'I'm casting no reflection on your capabilities, Mr. Brent — '

'Brett,' Mr. Brett corrected him with a thin smile, '*the* Martin Brett.'

'I beg your pardon, Mr. Brett. I was going to say I'm casting no — '

'You needn't give me the speech over again. You want real, live cops on the job. The Scotland Yard business.' Mr. Brett threw me a look. 'Let's not keep the gentleman waiting, tell 'em to come running.'

I picked up the bedside telephone and dialled the old familiar number. While I was being put through to the extension I wanted, the Harcourt girl suddenly piped up with:

'Mr. Palmer, I never knew you had a key to the flat.'

He looked at her with a faint smile. 'I didn't, till a moment ago. I found this in the door — after I'd been ringing.' He held out the palm of his hand to her and she took the key. 'You must have left it there,' he said. 'Careless of you, my dear.'

The girl stared at the key with a puzzled look for a moment, then started to dig into her handbag obviously unable to believe she hadn't retained the key. Her search seemed to be fruitless, however, because after a moment she looked up at the solicitor with a rueful expression. 'I'm afraid I must have done that,' she admitted.

I finished giving the Scotland Yard boy all the necessary details to start them moving fast in our direction and hung up. I looked at Mr. Brett and saw he was eyeing the solicitor with a chilly smile.

'Speaking of being careless,' he said to him suddenly, 'you've managed to make a mistake or two *yourself* this evening.' As Palmer opened his mouth to speak he went on urbanely as a cobra poised to strike. 'Save your breath, you're going to need it one of these early mornings, and I'll tell you what I mean. It goes like this: Waiting outside until you saw her' — with a nod at Mary Harcourt — 'go to the post, you slipped up here by *the stairs*. No doubt congratulating yourself you'd timed it just when the porter chanced to be off duty for a minute. You got into the flat by that key,' indicating the one the girl was holding, 'which you'd managed to get hold of somehow, then you knocked on this door in the usual way and Miss Dalby, unsuspecting, let you in. I can't tell you *why* you preferred her dead — could be you'd been monkeying around with her investments, it's been known to happen — but anyway when you'd done the job you hopped out through that window. You left it open deliberately to give the idea it was an outside job. Then you turn up here as expected. Any questions?'

'I've never heard such a preposterous rigmarole in all my life,' choked Palmer, but his face was beaded with sweat. He took out his handkerchief again. 'But as a matter of interest perhaps even a block-headed fool of a so-called detective such as you can offer some evidence for your wild, malicious accusation?'

Mr. Brett grinned at him over his cigarette. 'All right, as a matter of interest this prize chump will spill it. One, you forgot to lock the bedroom door behind you. Two, a minute ago you walked in here ... obviously knowing it wasn't locked, as it would have been had Miss Dalby been alive.'

There was a sudden gasp from the Harcourt girl and the porter as the significance of his words sank in. My eyes were on Palmer whose mouth was agape, his fingers clutching the handkerchief clenched convulsively.

'If you hadn't known she was dead,' Mr. Brett continued remorselessly, 'you would never have come barging in, you'd have waited for her to open the door.'

The solicitor darted a hunted look round the room, his mouth tightening into a thin line as he saw that the porter had moved forward and stood a tough, formidable figure between him and the door.

Mr. Brett read his thoughts. 'I shouldn't try it,' he said jeeringly. 'You might get hurt.'

Suddenly the other seemed to collapse like a deflated balloon. His control went to the winds and he broke out wildly: 'I didn't mean to do it. It was an accident. She struggled — it was an accident — '

The girl gave a horrified cry at this admission of guilt.

'Let me go. I'll pay anything. Anything — ' Palmer sobbed.

'Save it,' Mr. Brett told him coldly.

The other saved it and slumped a trembling, stricken figure, into a chair, burying his face in his hands. He stayed that way until the police arrived. As the Scotland Yard inspector — who was a personal friend of Mr. Brett's — was going, Mr. Brett took a Yale key from his pocket.

'By the way,' he said with typically elaborate casualness, 'you'll be wanting this.' To me who was gazing at it with certain curiosity he said: 'The Harcourt piece left it lying around when she came into the bedroom.'

'And Palmer made out she'd left it in the door,' I said.

He nodded. 'He had to talk his way out of being in possession of a key himself.'

He paused a moment reflectively, then muttered: 'Which reminds me. There's one angle of this case I *haven't* straightened yet.

I looked at him quizzically. It seemed to me he'd sewn up every aspect of the entire bag of tricks pretty neatly. I said:

'What would that trifling matter be, Mr. Brett?'

'Trifling matter, hell,' said Mr. Brett morosely. 'I've got to talk myself out of accepting that darned Scotland Yard cashier's usual mangy fee, and soak him for a *real* chunk of cash for a change.'

THE END

Books by Ernest Dudley
in the Linford Mystery Library:

ALIBI AND DR. MORELLE
THE HARASSED HERO
CONFESS TO DR. MORELLE
THE MIND OF DR. MORELLE
DR. MORELLE AND DESTINY
CALLERS FOR DR. MORELLE
LOOK OUT FOR LUCIFER!
MENACE FOR DR. MORELLE
NIGHTMARE FOR DR. MORELLE
THE WHISTLING SANDS
TO LOVE AND PERISH
DR. MORELLE TAKES A BOW
DR. MORELLE AND THE
DRUMMER GIRL
THE CROOKED STRAIGHT
MR. WALKER WANTS TO KNOW
TWO-FACE
DR. MORELLE AT MIDNIGHT
THE DARK BUREAU
THE CROOKED INN
THE BLIND BEAK
DR. MORELLE AND THE DOLL
LEATHERFACE

DR. MORELLE MEETS MURDER
A CASE FOR DR. MORELLE
DR. MORELLE'S CASEBOOK
DR. MORELLE INVESTIGATES
DR. MORELLE INTERVENES
SEND FOR DR. MORELLE
DR. MORELLE ELUCIDATES
DR. MORELLE MARCHES ON
MEET JIMMY STRANGE
ENTER JIMMY STRANGE
DEPARTMENT OF SPOOKS
NEW CASES FOR DR. MORELLE